Parenting Adhd

A Practical Positive Parenting Manual to Raise Happy and Successful Kids

(The Parents' Practical Guide to Their Newborn Baby)

Roderick Campbell

Published by Rob Miles

© Roderick Campbell

All Rights Reserved

*Parenting **Adhd:** A Practical Positive Parenting Manual to Raise Happy and Successful Kids (The Parents' Practical Guide to Their Newborn Baby)*

ISBN 978-1-990084-30-0

All rights reserved. No part of this guide may be reproduced in any form without permission in writing from the publisher except in the case of brief quotations embodied in critical articles or reviews.

Legal & Disclaimer

The information contained in this book is not designed to replace or take the place of any form of medicine or professional medical advice. The information in this book has been provided for educational and entertainment purposes only.

The information contained in this book has been compiled from sources deemed reliable, and it is accurate to the best of the Author's knowledge; however, the Author cannot guarantee its accuracy and validity and cannot be held liable for any errors or omissions. Changes are periodically made to this book. You must consult your doctor or get professional medical advice before using any of the suggested remedies, techniques, or information in this book.

Upon using the information contained in this book, you agree to hold harmless the Author from and against any damages, costs, and expenses, including any legal fees potentially resulting from the application of any of the information provided by this guide. This disclaimer applies to any damages or injury caused by the use and application, whether directly or indirectly, of any advice or information presented, whether for breach of contract, tort, negligence, personal injury, criminal intent, or under any other cause of action.

You agree to accept all risks of using the information presented inside this book. You need to consult a professional medical practitioner in order to ensure you are both able and healthy enough to participate in this program.

Table of Contents

INTRODUCTION 1

CHAPTER 1: HOW TO RAISE TODDLERS IN THE RIGHT WAY 2

CHAPTER 2: HOW TO CORRECTLY DISCIPLINE A CHILD? 6

CHAPTER 3: UNDERSTAND: IT'S NORMAL; IT'S A STAGE OF GROWTH 23

CHAPTER 4: APPLYING ZEN PARENTING MINDFUL APPROACH 30

CHAPTER 5: SIGN AND SYMPTOMS OF DYSLEXIA 42

CHAPTER 6: SIBLING RIVALRY: WHY IT HAPPENS 51

CHAPTER 7: WORTHWHILE ACTIVITIES FOR CHILDREN AT HOME 55

CHAPTER 8: EFFECTIVE PARENTING STRATEGIES FOR TODDLERS 60

CHAPTER 9: TERRIBLE TWOS AND THREES 66

CHAPTER 10: LOVE AND RESPECT 77

CHAPTER 11: ACCESS AND USAGE OF TOUCH SCREEN DEVICE BY CHILDREN 85

CHAPTER 12: DEALING WITH POWER STRUGGLES 97

CHAPTER 14: YOUR CHILD DOESN'T TALK TO YOU. EVER. ABOUT ANYTHING 111

CHAPTER 15: RUNNING A HOUSEHOLD AND FINDING A BALANCE 116

CHAPTER 15: RAISING YOUR CHILDREN 120

CHAPTER 16: DISCIPLINING TODDLERS 129

CHAPTER 17: POSITIVE PARENTING: WHAT IT IS AND WHAT IT ISN'T 140

CHAPTER 18: BATTLES TO OVERCOME AND POINTS TO PONDER 157

CHAPTER 19: THEY SEE THROUGH YOU 165

CHAPTER 20: PLAN ACTIVITIES WITH YOUR STEP CHILDREN 173

CHAPTER 21: PARENTING ACTIVITIES THAT AID IN POSITIVE FAMILIES 176

CHAPTER 22: IN A NUTSHELL 184

CHAPTER 23: THE WAY OUR MOMS AFFECT US 189

CONCLUSION 199

Introduction

Parenting isn't just about raising kids, but also developing characters that goes with buildingtheir social being. Mindless parenting can sabotage a child's progressiveness. Raising kids need to be envisioned from different aspects so as to make them well-rounded individuals and not to hamper their physical and mental growth.

This eBook on Conscious Parenting comes up with some astute suggestions and advices for raising your kids sensibly. Read this eBook carefully and learn from the suggestions given so you can give your child a healthy and an encouraging upbringing. Rear them, empower them and make them confident individuals!

Chapter 1: How To Raise Toddlers In The Right Way

Toddlers are the most vulnerable beings in this world. They are never aware of what they should do and only look up to the adults to be directed onto the right path. Well, the truth is that raising a toddler can be a really difficult job for a first time parent especially because they lack the experience of raising kids and it can prove a hard nut to crack.

Think about it; the toddler depends on you as a parent (whether this is your **1st** child or 20**th** child) for everything. They want to be fed, changed their diapers, taken to bed and even want you to understand them and always be there for them. They will wake you up in the middle of the night and not care whether you have to go to work or attend to anything else besides them. But even with all that, you need to learn what it is you MUST do to raise your child right.

Here is what you need to do:

Health

Monitor Your Child's Health

Toddlers do not know how to express what and how they are feeling to their parents. They may fall sick and if you are not careful or keen to notice, you probably won't even notice it at all! Well, as you well know, if this goes untreated, it could mean that you are putting the life of that child at risk. Although you might not be certain on what is troubling your child, you need to be keen to notice the signs that the child is sick. So what are these signs? You can tell that your child is sick if:

He or she cries a lot. Most kids cry a lot for various reasons but if you notice your child cries excessively (abnormally), he or she may be sick.

Has a fever. Fever in itself is not an illness. Rather, it a manifestation of an underlying illness. You should seek a doctor's help when you notice that your baby's temperature has fallen or raised abnormally.

Has difficulty in breathing. If your baby has difficulty in breathing, you should seek medical attention immediately. You can tell your child is experiencing breathing difficulties if he or she breathes more rapidly than usual, grunts while sleeping, the skin or tongue has bluish tinge or if he or she breathes with a hissing sound.

Has a cold: This can be exhibited by constant coughing.

Has rashes: Although rashes are fairly common in children, if you notice an increase in rashes on the baby's face, then it may be an indication that the baby is sick so you should seek medical advice

Appears pale and dehydrated

Has diarrhea or is vomiting consistently

Your child (toddler) cannot talk much about what he or she is feeling. As such, it is upon you to seek medical attention for your child immediately. The earlier you do that, the better for you-in any case, it is always better to be safe than sorry. Well, even as you try to restore your child's health, it is important to keep in mind that that there are some things you shouldn't do when your child is sick.

What not to do when your child falls sick:

Prescribe over the counter drugs for your kid. Unless you are a doctor, you should never prescribe any drugs for your child. You should be very sure what your child is suffering from before giving him or her any drugs and this should be only done after seeking proper medical attention for your child.

Giving your child some foods that you believe will make him better. Some parents believe that if they give their kids certain foods while sick, they will get well. I do not totally disagree with these myths but the best solution is to take your child to a doctor. Most of these foods do not make everyone feel better and you should never assume anything that is not scientifically proven.

Chapter 2: How To Correctly Discipline A Child?

Parenting is a broad term that involves adopting unique and diverse methods, techniques, and skills to raise a child successfully. It is a tough job that begins immediately when the child is born until he is ready to stand on his own feet. The enormous responsibility to mold a tiny infant into a healthy and well-rounded individual lies in your hand.

As the child grows older, the responsibility becomes more prominent and more challenging, especially when it is time to exercise your duty to discipline him. As this period commences, you face the pressure to build an open, healthy, and quality relationship with your child, while being firm about the rules and expectations that you set. It is crucial to approach parenting with laser focus like you do when completing a job or working to achieve success if you want to ensure that your child grows well-mannered, disciplined, and responsible.

The Goals of Parenting

Not all people are bestowed with a privilege to become parents, robbing them of the incredible opportunity associated with child-raising. When it happens, this life-changing event motivates you to become a better version of yourself- more loving, more patient, more responsible, more generous, and a lot more, all for the sake of your child.

There are three fundamental goals that all parents across the world share.

Ensuring the child's health and safety.

Preparing the child to become a productive adult.

Transmitting cultural values.

The desire to provide and protect their children at all times is inherent to all parents. It is essential, especially when your child is still an infant. Children need caring in a way that ensures their survival and protect them against harm. Parents must give children the best possible start in life- the best care, education, and food.

As a parent, you act on his behalf, shielding your child against all kinds of threats. Rushing to comfort your child at the first sign of disappointment or stopping him from trying new things because you are afraid that he might get hurt can cause more harm than good. Some parents attempt to push their children toward particular paths, but allowing them to find their own life goals is the essence of effective parenting. There will come a time that you need to start allowing the child begins his journey, and you as a figure of authority, to begin teaching him the value of discipline. The earlier you establish certain limits for your child, the higher the percentage that he will grow into a responsible adult.

One of the challenges that parents face is how to raise a well-disciplined child without hindering his happy and healthy journey into adulthood. Discipline is vital to every family. Its goal is to help children learn self-control and choose acceptable behavior. However, it is necessary to remember that every child is born with a unique DNA that influences his temperament, character, and personality.

What is Discipline?

Discipline is described as a strategy to train someone to obey a code of behavior or rules. It is the process of demonstrating what kind of behavior is acceptable and what is not.

When you establish house rules like no watching television or using tablet until homework is done, no video games during school days, no hurtful teasing, or name-calling when playing with other siblings, you are training your child to develop self-control and understand your expectations. Simple house rules shape your child's behavior. You are teaching him the basic skills on how to manage his behavior. It is important to start while he is young to prepare him against the challenges and demands of the outside world, especially during learning years in school.

Take note that as your kid grows, his behavior changes as he goes through development. It may surprise you one day when he throws tantrums all of a sudden or become hard-headed. All behavioral changes are part of growing up, each age and stage give the child certain struggles that you, as a parent, need to understand. You need to guide him in processing these changes by not resorting to yelling, threatening, or imposing punishment.

Hence, the importance of choosing a disciplinary approach that focuses on finding the right balance. It must blend well with your parenting style, helping you feel in control without affecting the optimum development of your child's physical, mental, and emotional development. One of the approaches that can help you discipline your child without losing your self-control and maintain a healthy, loving, respectful relationship with him is **Positive Discipline**.

A. POSITIVE DISCIPLINE

Wikipedia describes Positive Discipline as a type of discipline model that focuses on the child's positive behavior. It is based on the concept that there are no bad children, only bad behaviors. Other related teachings include:

Good behaviors can be taught and reinforced. Bad behaviors can be corrected and modified without hurting them physically or emotionally.

Verbal punishment is sometimes more damaging than physical punishment, leaving children insecure, anxious, or fearful.

Positive Discipline aims to promote family togetherness, cooperation, and treating each other with respect. It is geared to encouraging parents to train their children in making good choices, solve problems, and make agreements that foster creativity and critical thinking. It does not rely on punishments or rewards. Instead, it utilizes the power of empathy, active listening, relationship building, and mutual respect to develop positive behaviors.

It is focused on:

Non-punitive solutions

Respectful and non-violent interactions

Identifying the meaning behind the behavior

Effective and clear communication

Building self-esteem and capability

Encouragement (instead of praise)

Connection and Play

Finding long-term solutions to develop self-discipline

Mutually respectful parent and child relationship

Teaching lifelong skills

Increases confidence and competence to handle difficult situations

This approach is not new. It became popular in the 1920s when psychologists Dr. Alfred Adler and Dr. Rudolf Dreikurs introduced the idea of positive discipline to the audiences in the United States. Dr. Adler focused his attention on parenting education, actively teaching parents to treat their children with respect. He also argued that pampering and spoiling children could result in behavioral and social problems. Thus he advocated against them. The classroom management techniques were initially introduced during the same period in Vienna, Austria. However, it was only in the late 1930s that Dr. Dreikurs brought it to the U.S.

Their advocacy became the basis of Positive Discipline, an approach that is designed and developed by Dr. Jane

Nelsen to help parents, mentors, and other authorities raise responsible, resilient, and independent children. It teaches essential life and social skills in a manner or approach that maintains mutual respect and encourages a deeper understanding of the discipline.

Techniques Used in Positive Discipline

Technique 1: Creating Rules

Dr. Nelsen emphasizes the significance of establishing clear and reasonable rules. She recommends that as much as possible, rules are devised by children with the guidance of parents of authority figure and agreed upon by everyone. It will make them more accountable to follow the rules. If there is a need to modify the rules or introduce a new one, make sure that your child is informed about it and understand the reasons for the modification.

Technique 2: Recognizing Needs

Another theory that governs Positive Discipline is that when the child misbehaves, he is displaying an unmet need that requires satisfaction. It is necessary to focus on recognizing and meeting the need instead of the behavior itself to deal with the misbehavior.

Technique 3: Redirecting Negative Behavior

It is best to encourage positive behavior by redirecting the child's attention to something interesting and creative to resolve or stop the acts of misbehavior.

Technique 4: Understanding the Meaning

Sometimes, misbehavior or acting out is the child's way to get attention from his parents or other people around him. It is essential to understand that children, like adults, do not do something without a valid reason. Once you understand the trigger that caused the behavior, remove or resolve it to prevent further emotional outbursts from your kid.

Technique 5: Inspiring Intrinsic Motivation

Intrinsic motivation refers to the inherent desire of a person to feel good about oneself. The motivation comes from within and not from external sources, that include getting a reward or avoiding punishment.

All these techniques encourage the behaviors you want to see while discouraging the behaviors that you do not want to manifest in your child. In positive parenting, it is important to maintain a respectful, positive relationship with the child, while trying to decrease or increase the behavior. When things get frustrating and challenging along the way- keep your cool.

Easier said than done, right? But, when you focus on the long-term results, you will eventually say that all your efforts paid off. For now, it helps to focus on the principles of positive discipline, one day at a time. It will help you find solutions to behavioral problems, instead of temporarily stopping the problems.

The good news is- Positive Discipline is effective. Based on studies and surveys, children perform and behave better when they perceive both kindness and firmness from the parents. With high responsiveness to the feelings and needs, while setting realistic and high expectations, parents motivate children to work on concrete goals, become academically and socially successful, and less likely to engage in risky behaviors.

B. PARENTING STATISTICS

According to the National Parent Survey of Zero to Three.Org., seventy-three (73%) of parents say that parenting becomes their biggest life challenge.

Eighty-three percent (83%) believed that positive and effective parenting strategies could be learned.

Sixty-nine percent (69%) of parents said that if they knew about positive discipline techniques, they would use them to become better parents.

Fifty-four percent (54%) of parents wished that they had access to the information on how to become better fathers and mothers.

The demographics showed that parents of various circumstances and backgrounds have strikingly similar beliefs about the joys and challenges of parenting. Almost everyone claimed that they are good parents. There is also a universal, intense desire to improve their parenting techniques and skills.

A whopping ninety-one (91%) claimed that becoming parents is their greatest joy.

Eighty-percent percent (80%) of parents from various income and education levels, races, or ethnicities strongly agreed that they are good parents to their kids.

Eighty-seven percent (87%) stated that they work hard to become better parents.

Seventy percent (70%) said that their lives changed when they became parents.

On Child Discipline

One of the dilemmas that parents face is how to discipline their kids. Every couple or parent has a parenting style that includes discipline strategies, which they believe are the most effective approach. Most often, they mimic or diversify their own parents' techniques.

Sixty-eight percent (68%) say that they use discipline to stop the bad behaviors of their children.

About fifty-seven percent (57%) are trying to figure out the best strategy to discipline their growing kids.

Fifty-six percent (56%) admit that managing their children during the acts of misbehavior is a real challenge.

In the context of terrifying kids as a form of discipline, there are many debates and controversies that revolve around it because of its adverse and abusive effects on children. It is important to pay attention to several factors such as intergenerational modeling, respect/embarrassment, and power/fear to understand why a lot of parents use this strategy.

Intergenerational modeling refers to the frame of reference that new parents adapt. Typically, they copy the parenting style of their parents or other influential people around them.

Respect/embarrassment pertains to the desire of the parents to be in control and be respected. Any form of disobedience is viewed as a sign of disrespect.

Power/fear is about the fear of parents that the behavior of their children will endanger or harm them. To ensure that their kids blend in well without being noticed or prevent being hurt (physically or emotionally), they instill fear to terrifying them.

Thirty-seven percent (37%) admit that they spank their children.

Thirty-two percent (32%) yell to their children.

Twenty-nine percent (29%) say they swat or pop their children.

Twenty-eight percent (28%) hit them with an object.

Twenty-three percent (23%) intentionally embarrass them.

Sixteen percent (16%) force them to do a rigorous activity as a form of punishment.

On Physical Abuse

There is a thin line that separates discipline and abuse. Every year, approximately 3 million cases of child abuse are reported. Another long-term adult study showed that 14.8% reported that they are physically abused, 12.2% are sexually abused, and 25.9% are verbally abused. Many abused children grow up with poor health and struggling against alcoholism, drug addiction, depression, mental illness, and traumas.

According to the Centers for Disease Control and Prevention, experiences of abuse and neglect during childhood result to health problems of adults. It was summarized by the World Health Organization (WHO) by stating that household dysfunction and childhood maltreatment are significant factors to the development of chronic diseases (during the later years), which are the common causes of disability and death in the United States.

One form of child maltreatment is physical abuse, which can be intentional or unintentional and can harm his health, development, survival, dignity, or self-esteem. It includes beating, hitting, shaking, kicking, suffocating, boxing ears, biting, strangling, and fatal acts like poisoning, forced ingestion, scalding, or burning.

Most physical violence against children happens inside the premise of homes, with the intent to punish them. In the U.S. alone, a large number of parents admitted that they resort to physical abuse as a form of corporal punishment to correct their kids' bad behaviors. In cases that the ordinary physical punishment becomes escalated, turning into mild to severe maltreatment or abuse, the contributory factors include parent's inability to judge their strength or control anger as well as being unaware of the vulnerability of their kids.

Chapter 3: Understand: It's Normal; It's A

Stage Of Growth

Your sweet angel just embarrassed you in a restaurant and you had to take a walk of shame out because everyone was staring at 'the screaming child' whose parent could not get them to shut up. You are now getting into deep negotiations with that 2year old child, about what they want to do and what you want and why your way can't work. I mean it's exhausting.

Sometimes it's easy to think these to be sigs of a rebellious and disrespectful individual. Where I grew up, this would earn some serious spanking – to get that demon out (bad behavior was termed as a demon). If a child misbehaved, it was due to lack of spanking. That is what traditional parents did; most of us who are parents now grew up that way.

I would not call it backward thinking because our parents really did instill discipline in their ways and it worked. However, this is not the best way to deal with a 2 year old. They are not being hard headed - at least not on purpose. That child does not even know that they are being difficult.

But why are they portraying difficult behavior?

What Is Really Happening?

They are not born with social skills

Experts in neurology say that a child is born with a clean slate. They have no pre-programmed way to think or feel – they learn from their environment. In other words, they learn from their caregiver – you.

Do you know what they do in the mean time? They live by the famous 'survival for the fittest' jungle rule; it's the natural and automatic mentality they come into the world with. They do not know patience, humility, negotiation skills or any appropriate way of asking for what they want. This is why they will bite, scratch, scream and hit just to prove a point – like a panda would do in the forest.

Its development

Toddler years are a time of growth. This is when they develop a sense of self; they realize that 'hey, I am here, really do exist". This comes with having personal desires, feelings, thoughts and needs that sometimes the parent is not able to read or understand like they did before. Also, they now have opinions and a certain level of reasoning (but they do not realize it's flawed).

The kid wants to do certain things for themselves; they wants things to happen in a certain manner and when they are unable to, it results to frustration – thus the tantrums.

They have a limited ability to communicate or to do

The thing is; they do not have the language skills to express themselves or explain why they do not want certain things or even ask for help; in their mind, they have tried in the best way possible to make you understand or they have strained their ability to do something, say make a toy bike stand, and it won't.

The only way they think of letting out their frustration is what we like to call temper tantrums. The gap between want/desire and ability to do/have results in those unruly behaviors associated with 'terrible twos'.

Lack of self-consciousness and flawed reasoning

Every one of us is opinionated, including the toddler. We want people to hear us and at least consider our opinions or desires. The only difference between everyone else and a toddler is self-consciousness; being self-aware. A toddler doesn't care where they are or who they are with and under what circumstances. They simply know they are here and that they have a desire or a principle that is being violated and they will do whatever it takes to have them addressed.

They are slaves to their moods

We all have moods but a grownup is able to get a grip of their emotions. A toddler will swing wherever the moods drive them. Sometimes they are hungry, tired, bored or sleepy – some of the major triggers of moodiness. They will then have a melt down because they cannot contain the pangs of hunger or their heavy eyes – not because they are bothersome.

It means that you are in charge

'Terrible twos' is what many call this toddler phase. Rest assured that it will not be fun. There are days you will want to cry, scream and throw stuff yourself from the frustration they put you through. However, if you take it positively, which you should, you will realize that your child is not being bothersome, but they are developing and learning – which is a good sign. The unruly behavior is their way of testing boundaries to figure out right from wrong – which is dependent on your response.

It's all a learning experience – and the lessons they take from here will mould them into the type of individual that they will become in future. It is important to understand that even in the midst of their craziest tantrums, the child is looking up to you for guidance and support.

This is why you cannot be absorbed in their tantrums; you have to guide. Sure, it's challenging but it's the way you handle the challenges you are experiencing with your child which shapes how they turn out from this phase onwards. The next chapters are dedicated to giving you expert advice on the right way to deal with all the challenges of toddler years.

Chapter 4: Applying Zen Parenting

Mindful Approach

As a parent it is crucial to develop a Zen like mind which requires an understanding that when we get upset because of our children's indiscipline acts, and refusal of taking up responsibilities, our temper which results to yelling and arguing with the child should instead be harnessed into positive acts as demonstrated by the Eight mindful steps of Zen. The mindful steps are guidance on how to instill responsibility and discipline in a peaceful manner. In Zen, it is argued that spanking is not a bad punishment but if discipline can be achieved through other ways, then why not? This will lead to happiness for you and your child. Let us apply these steps in our parenting styles:

Understand your child

Who is a child? What do they go through? Why do they make mistakes? You should often ask yourself these questions in order to have the right understanding of your child and the environment, which affects their behavior. Children are fragile beings who are still unaware of many things in their environment. Taking your time to understand them and the reasons as to why they misbehave will enable you to be in charge of the situation and guide them in the right path to take. For instance, you may want to punish your child because of not doing their homework; sitting them down and listening to their explanation may be the solution because you may find out that your child is a slow learner who needs to be taught using a different technique for them to acquire the necessary knowledge.

When children get parents who understand them, they are able to do their best not to disappoint the parents in any way. Understand your child and you will know the kind of discipline to give and responsibilities that they are capable of handling.

Good intentions are worthwhile

As a parent, you should develop a mind full of pure intentions. This involves having positive thoughts of your child. You should work towards what you know are the right things to do. Power struggles and yelling are not in the list and so should be avoided in whichever circumstance. Choosing to overlook your child's mistakes by not punishing them is one way. This will be a practice of forgiveness however; this should not deter you from mentioning the mistake they have made and correcting them while smiling at them. Show love and kindness to your child. By doing this, you will get fulfillment as the child will show their love and obedience towards you.

Tame your speech

Words that we use have much weight in bringing up your children. It can either motivate or kill our children's morale and confidence. We should therefore learn to have positive talks in guiding our children towards responsibilities. Positive words like "you are good", "you are bright" and "you are beautiful" enable your child to appreciate him or herself and approach life in a positive way. Speech should also be accompanied by being honest, avoid lies as when you lie, you will have to cover it up with more lies but when you tell the truth, you won't have to repeat it over. Being truthful to your words will ensure that you get respect from your child. The child will also adapt that policy hence provide true accountability for their actions.

Actions

Teach your child to act in the right way by also ensuring that you act in the right way so that they can learn from your example. In addition, your pure actions will encourage your child to cultivate goodness in their behavior, as they will see there is more gain in being disciplined and responsible. Make sure you also portray hard work and morale when carrying out your chores. For instance, going to work in the morning should be an enjoyable thing so that your child may also be passionate about school. Ensure you don't curse each time you wake up in the morning and complain at how much you hate your job as this will rub your children the wrong way.

Embrace Mindfulness

We are accustomed to judging our children by the way they behave. Mindfulness does not support this act but instead incorporates the act of creating awareness for ourselves and monitoring our children with the sole purpose of helping them where they fall short. Judging and misinterpreting our children's actions should not be in our thoughts. Look at your child in their present circumstances and keep off from reminding yourself of how they should behave. This will help calm yourself in the moment of intense pressure and calmness will lead to making of sound decisions that will affect your child positively. For instance, just because your child broke a glass while washing utensils last week does not mean that they are prone to do the same this week, so when they handle a glass, keep your distance to enable them take the responsibility of washing, wiping and putting it in the cabinet.

Embrace Meditation

In meditation, you achieve full concentration that calms your mind and gives you insight of how to handle every situation that your child might put you through. It also deters you from engaging in power struggles with your child as you will not be in the capacity to exchange verbal confrontations. In meditation, you learn to control your breathing and pressure, clearing off your mind from the stress of parenting. When you apply this every time your child behaves in an inappropriate manner, it will make your child know that they are hurting you deeply and seeing you don't want to quarrel with them, they will pull back from misbehaving as they sometimes do it intentionally to annoy you.

Have the right work environment

You might be thinking how your work environment affects your child. We work in order to provide for our children and may even result to taking on more than one job to earn that extra cash. In Zen, the way you earn your living could affect your child's behavior to a larger extent. You should ensure that you earn a living from a profession that you are proud of. That is the only way that you will achieve happiness and you will in turn treat your child with such. For instance, if you are involved in drug trafficking, this would mean that at times, you will have to bring some drugs to the house for packaging and delivery. Remember your child may be watching you at that time, in their curiosity, they might take some and after a while become drug addicts. Parents who also act as sex workers and use their homes as the venue contribute to negative upbringing of the child. These jobs usually come with lots of frustrations that may lead you to abusing your own child.

Instead, it becomes better to earn little from doing jobs that don't cause any harm. In any case, how will you tell your child not to sell drugs or do other heinous acts when you are involved in such acts?

Let your efforts be seen

Without the right effort, it will be impossible to practice Zen parenting. Parenting is very difficult especially when you juggle between success in your home and at work. You need to understand that parenting needs our dedication, patience, tolerance, and stability for it to bring out positive results. Having the right effort will motivate you and help you to realize your child is about to make a mistake and correct them in advance. In practicing positive efforts, you should reward your child with a gift when they portray a positive behavior or show improvement in their behavior. For instance, if your child used to fail at doing chores, when they change their mindset and show the willingness to perform their duties without much struggle, a reward will be a way of telling them that you are impressed by the change of scenario.

Apart from the mindful path, these extra tips on Zen Habits will indeed make you stand out as a parent when incorporated together.

Put yourself in their shoes

Imagine at that point of your life, when things are not going your way, you get fired at your job, bills are piling up to be paid, what would you require from other people. The obvious answer is love, patience and understanding. You won't appreciate it at all when your parents start yelling at you, calling you irresponsible but will be in control when they come forth and support you in that particular situation. That is also the way you should treat your children for them to grow responsibly and with discipline given that at times, they go through difficult situations when growing up and they need your understanding and not your condemnation.

Don't put yourself in the equation

As a parent, you have to remind yourself that when your kids are on the wrong, it is not usually about you, but the situation or circumstance they are going through. Don't assume that they are doing things intentionally to annoy you or to get back at you for not giving them what they want. When we do this, we tend to become angry and react by shouting or yelling. By learning to act objectively, you will be in a position to see clearly and use the right efforts such as positive thinking to bring out the best in your child's situation.

Guide them

We need our kids to be able to make sound decisions on their own. I support coming up with rules that should be adhered to at home. However, by setting down rules that are to be followed, the children may grow up depending on someone to tell them what to and what not to do. Remember you may not be with your child all the time. Once they are all grown up, they will have to leave home to go to college and so forth. Therefore, the trick is to guide them in following the rules by explaining to them the basics of life and how to apply that for the betterment of their future. In guidance, you act as their mentor which is good as they will copy your behaviors.

Walk away

At that time when the children have upset you to the point you feel as though you may do something that you will regret, it is always advisable to calm down before you express yourself to them. You need to breathe, as at that time it is difficult to think straight. Sound decisions are made when we have cooled off.

Accept reality

Being mindful enables us to be aware that we are bound to make mistakes from time to time. What matters in the end is how we deal with our mistakes. You should try to control your emotions, be compassionate and able to instill discipline in your children in the right way as life is a series of ups and downs.

I believe that the Eight fold path of Zen is now embedded in you. Remember, practice makes perfect so do not tire if you are not able to do it right at the start.

To couple it up, let's look at mistakes that we make when instilling discipline so as to make a change in ourselves.

Chapter 5: Sign And Symptoms Of Dyslexia

Dyslexic child may have severe or mild impairment. Symptoms and sign may vary depending on the situation and environment involved. These are the following signs of dyslexia:

☐ Problems in pronouncing words

☐ Talking later than other child

☐ Encounter difficulty in rhyming words

☐ Difficulty in learning basics such as numbers, colors and even alphabets.

☐ Handwriting problems and unrefined motor skills

☐ Confusion on letters and order of it

☐ Problem in learning the connection between letters and their sounds.

Older children or adults may have the following signs:

Trouble in schoolwork

Poor handwriting skills

Encounter difficulty in remembering numbers and letters

Difficulty in following sequences or directions.

Problem in writing, spelling and reading

Problem in learning foreign languages

Main Causes of Dyslexia

Experts do not know what exactly cause of dyslexia but they found out that genetics play a major role in it. If you and your partner have dyslexia, your children have the higher risk to have the disorder. Dyslexia tends to run in the path of families and the researchers conclude that genes may be responsible for this condition.

Scientist also found brain difference which is involved in dyslexia. This shows that dyslexia may results from certain structural varieties of brain specifically the left hemisphere.

Dyslexic people's brain show very little activity in areas where in written form of words relied. So in order in to read, they must develop alternative neurological path ways of learning. They make use of Broca's area which is associated with the other phases of language, speech and writing.

Dyslexic Treatment

Even your child is under this condition, there are a lot of things that can be done to help them survived. Dyslexia is not a disease, it can be cured and manage. Dyslexic child can benefit enormously in getting special education attention. Your child will be able to achieve his full potentials and talents if you will show him support and concerns in his everyday life.

Dyslexic child need to be up headed in special schools wherein they are the focus of the school and their attention are considered brilliant. They just need an extra help coming from you as their parent. Teachers and doctors can help you in managing your child's potentials and capabilities. They will guide you and give advice about your child's needs necessities.

Self-Esteem

Children with dyslexia may face different challenges emotionally. The unwavering support concern coming from a parent is critical. Encouragement and support to develop special potentials children is part of building self –esteem and self love. The confidence and self-esteem develop from real can be one way to succeed. Praise your child for hard work and show willingness in helping him and learn more and better. Show him the importance of right attitudes and traits that will lead him to self reliance and self success. The main point of giving child homework is to reinforce what was taught in the classroom and how high the child learned.

Dyslexic children perform better when the teachers gives them a list of to do task. The completion of this task motivates the child to do better.

Knowledge

As their parent, you should educate yourself about dyslexia. The department on your child's school should have special education to sustain the needs of children. Ask the administrators if the

teachers are all trained and well in handling dyslexic children. Since the teachers are the primary advocates, you should ensure that these advocators are all knowledgeable enough to handling certain condition. The more you know, the better equipped you will help your child's performance in school.

Support

You should find a back up support to secure help for your child in the classroom. You can join groups and organization which aimed to help and guide parents in learning such abilities. These organizations teach methods to help dyslexic children in further assistance and support.

Ways of Coping with Dyslexia

There are a lot of ways on how you can help your child to cope with dyslexia.

Let your child to know that he has a bigger brain than the other.

Help your child to understand that he has a bigger brain than other. Their brain's right hemisphere is about 10% larger.

Remind your child that even though he's dyslexic he is still smart.

Always remind your child that his condition is not a hindrance to excel and succeed. In fact, dyslexic children can learn more effectively.

Never let your child to feel frustrated

Whenever your child encountered frustration, give him your support and show him that he has nothing to worry about.

Teach your child to use the graphic organizers and chart.

This will surely help your child in taking lessons and studying.

Have a connection with other parents.

It will be better if you can learn other learning techniques from the other parents. You will surely learn techniques and strategies to make your child more successful learner.

Talk your child about Dyslexia and Explain everything about it.

Since your children suffer from this condition, he has the tendency to ask you lots of questions about his condition. It will be better to let them know all about their conditions. It will help them to fully understand their position and condition. Here are some questions that you may encounter:

What do you mean by dyslexia?

Your child knows the term but he's not aware about the definition of this. Tell your child that it is a difficulty in learning.

How does it happen that I was born dyslexia?

Answer him in a positive way. "You were born with this condition, just like when you were born with blue eyes, pink cheeks,etc."

Is my brain abnormal and dysfunctional?

"No. Your brain has a different learning system. You have the difficulty in reading and it will take longer for you to learn but as time goes by, you'll learn to read and write just like other children."

Is it contagious?

"No. It's not contagious. It's not a virus."

Does it really mean I'm stupid?

"No. Dyslexia is difficulty in reading but it doesn't mean you are stupid. It has nothing to do with your intelligence."

Is it forever with me? Will it go away?"

"No. But you will surely learn to read. You just have to take patience and courage. You are not the problem. Sooner or later, you will learn how to cope with your condition"

Am I abnormal?

"No. You are special creation of our Almighty God."

Chapter 6: Sibling Rivalry: Why It Happens

Parents with more than one child often worry that their children will not get along; that they will argue with each other. That is the very definition of sibling rivalry and contrary to popular belief, a fair and healthy amount of sibling rivalry is good for your children and family.

Many experts use the term sibling rivalry to describe the infighting, competition, and jealousy that normally happens between siblings (brothers and sisters—blood or otherwise).

As I have hinted at above, sibling rivalry in healthy doses is good for the children because it is a coping mechanism. However, when the rivalry surpasses healthy levels, you can bet that it will have a negative effect on the family unit.

With that said, you should understand that—and this is why we said that some level of sibling rivalry is healthy—any family that has more than one child will have some level of sibling rivalry going on at some level. A parent's job is to keep the peace and ensure the rivalry is healthy for his or her children, their growth, and their interpersonal skills.

Experts have hinted that sibling rivalry starts long before, or after the birth of the second child. If not checked, the rivalry can last a very long time—sometimes even into adulthood—because as children grow up, their needs change and the changes can have a significant effect on the relationship.

As we have also hinted, because a family is a unit, when siblings fight and quarrel, when there is sibling rivalry, it affects everyone in the family but in particular you as the parent because when you do not know how to handle rivalry, it can lead to a lot of stress and frustration.

While I will have an in-depth look at why sibling rivalry happens, we can say now that as we have hinted, positive rivalry can have good effect. For instance, when siblings engage in healthy competition, it can improve grades and overall performance.

However, when siblings feel the need to compete for resources and in some cases, attention from parents, the rivalry and jealousy that develops from this can have an adverse effect on the relationship and affect the family dynamic. This is the kind of rivalry you have to guard against and equip your children with strategies to overcome.

With the above stated, it is worth mentioning here that your role is not to stop all infighting. As we have said, healthy arguments and disagreements are one of the best ways through which children learn to respect each other, practice fairness, and resolve differences in an amicable way. This is very beneficial because if you show them how to do it the right way, you will ensure that they can argue and disagree without resorting to violence.

Now that we have a fairer understanding of what sibling rivalry is, let us discuss some of its main causes:

Chapter 7: Worthwhile Activities For Children At Home

Parents choose to stay at home with their children so they can spend quality time with them. Some work-from home mothers would definitely resort to giving kids toys to play with. This could work however, children could also get bored easily, especially if they are already familiar with the toys and have played with it countless of times before. So what else can parents do to keep the kids preoccupied other than letting them watch and stare at the television for hours?

Here are some worthwhile activities to keep children busy at home:

"Sumo" wrestling

This activity is good for ages 5 and up. King-size pillows plus Dad's old T-shirts are the only things needed. Wrap the pillows around the kid (front and back) then let them wear their Dad's old shirt. Let them wrestle and use all their energy bouncing off each other "sumo" wrestling style. This can help the kid channel his hyper and rambunctious energy the fun and safe way.

Magic Pictures

This activity is recommended for children ages 1-2 years. Things needed are markers, crayons, masking tape and paper. To start the activity, draw a lot of things or letters of the alphabet on sheets of paper. There should be one drawing for every sheet of paper. It could be a house, a letter, a shape or an animal. Follow the shape and cover it with a masking tape. Let the kids color the entire page (except the picture covered with the tape). Once done coloring the entire page, let them carefully remove the tape and show them the picture beneath. This can keep them preoccupied and interested for long periods of time.

Fortress Building

This activity is good for children ages 5 and up.

Need to get the dinner ready? Give the kids a pile of pillows, blankets and bed sheets and let them be creative on their own. They can build a fort using the living room couch or the table and chairs for anchors. Once construction is done, give them flashlights and let them do shadow puppets. Show them some hand patterns and let them follow. This can make them occupied until supper.

Impromptu Hide and Seek

This activity is good for kids ages 4 and up. Children especially like playing hide and seek. This time, they will be looking for hidden objects around the house. So if there's a lot of work to do at home or a lot of articles to write, make sure to hide as many interesting objects as possible. Give them the list and let them search for it around the house. Be prepared to clean the mess after because this activity can really get messy having things thrown all over the place. Knowing how kids are...this will definitely keep them interested for hours. Make sure that they will be getting a corresponding prize for every object they will find to keep it more fun.

Collage-making

This activity is good for ages 3 and up. Things needed are old magazines (make sure they are colourful), blank paper (cartolina or Manila paper will do) and some glue sticks or paste. Now, set the kids up and give them the colourful magazines and let them rip every page they like. Don't just let them rip anything. Give them some themes like, pictures with water, summer pictures, toys, or grandma. Have them pick the photos they like best. Let them stick these pictures to a scrap or blank paper and leave them to themselves. This one's guaranteed to keep them busy for hours. It's fun and creative at the same time.

Cut-out pictures

This activity is good for children 6 and up. Things you will need are scissors, sheets of paper, magazines, and glue. Make sure the scissors are child-friendly and not those kinds of scissors which are big, heavy and made of metal. There are scissors made of plastic and are really made for children. Let them browse some old books or magazines, and have them cut the pictures they pick. Give them a theme, for example, a girl in the city, or school or nature. Then let them arrange all the cut-out pictures and stick them to a blank paper.

Make sure the pictures are well suited for the theme and then let them create a story out of the pictures they cut. Children will definitely love this activity because they love storytelling. It can also be in a form of a flip chart, or a self-made paper television. It can also be used for puppet-making. Just put some strings on the cut-out pictures and create a small stage. Let them play with their own creativity and they will surely love the activity and leave their parents doing their own thing.

Chapter 8: Effective Parenting Strategies

For Toddlers

In most cases, life tends to be frustrating for toddlers. Although eager to be self-governing, toddlers don't have the prowess to move as swiftly as they want or express what they desire. Children experience difficulties when coping with disappointments, limits, and compromise. These struggles can result in misbehaviors and tantrums. However, you can train your toddler to behave well by showering him or her with love, providing clear rules, and delivering predictable routines. In this book, we'll discuss the most effective parenting strategies to deescalate tantrums, handle challenges, and help your child grow socioemotionally. You'll also learn how to address tantrums and emotional children and acquire effective strategies to help your child obtain resilience.

Introduction: Effective Parenting

Effective parenting is important as it allows you to raise responsible and mentally healthy children. Parenting is an exciting task but extremely arduous at the same time. You have the responsibility of teaching your children all the things you know, but you need to make the right decisions at the same time. Every parent has unique parenting challenges and learning curves. Thus, parenting definitely entails a trial and error process.

Sometime, you might make a wrong decision or feel like you're not the kind of a parent you need to be. If this happens, all you have to do is make decisions that will transform your parenting style. From that point, you'll then be able to be an effective parent.

As a parent, you're human and prone to making mistakes from time to time. You might say some wrong things, make poor choices, or even show up at the incorrect time. At times, your child will yell at you, make fun of you, and get frustrated by your actions. All these reactions and mistakes are par for the parenting process. Never try to be a perfect mother or father since this isn't achievable. After all, you don't have to be a perfect parent to be an effective parent. All the mistakes, blunders, and mishaps help you teach your children valuable life lessons.

Instead, your core goal as an effective parent is to raise a responsible and mentally healthy child who will be ready to face life's realities as he or she grows. Here are some helpful tips to serve as an effective parent:

Enforcing the rules

Boundaries and house rules play a vital role in keeping you insane and help a growing child feel stable and secure. You need to be clear about what the child is allowed to do, the duties that he or she must finish, and how one must treat other people in the house. The child can make misstep occasionally. After you give him or her instructions, try to remind your child about the consequences if one makes a mistake. Just calmly reiterate, "If you don't collect the toys, you won't get the candy."

Being flexible

When enforcing home rules, avoid being extremely strict, and try to be flexible in some situations. Making numerous rules might backfire, and this might be dangerous to children. A study conducted by the University of New Hampshire indicated that children raised by overly strict parents tend to break the rules more often. The finding further indicates that children reared with strict parents tend to exhibit low self-esteem and a reduced sense of self-worth than those with less strict parents. Your child needs to know the repercussions of failing to follow the rules.

Talking to your children

Effective communication is extremely essential if you want to be an effective parent. Even if your child is learning how to babble, he or she benefits from active conversations with you. Talk about everything. Ask your child how the day was at school, or even what he or she wants for the next birthday. Long conversations help children to learn about language, imaginative thinking, and social languages.

As an effective parent, you must allow your children to face challenges. While adversity facilitates character building, there are some situations where the little one will need your assistance. As he or she grows, you can let your child start to conquer the challenges on one's own. Remember to explain that it's ok to fail sometimes and then motivate your child to continue honing one's skills.

The strategy is imperative as it lets children know that their parents won't always be around to help them. Kids also learn to recognize that sometimes things might not go the way they desire, but that isn't a reason to give up. Remind your child that he or she can deal with uncomfortable feeling in a healthy way that can lead to tantrums such as failure and rejection in

Chapter 9: Terrible Twos And Threes

Who has your baby become, and why is he driving you crazy? While your child's behaviors may seem terrible from time to time, what appears to be dreadful to you is really normal and healthy for your child. Your child is not intentionally trying to drive you crazy, but is trying out her new-found power and independence.

What occurs at around 18 months of age is that your baby begins to realize that he is not physically part of you but is instead a distinctly individual being with control over his own destiny. She has recently begun to walk, opening up new opportunities and horizons. He has a rapidly increasing repertoire of play, communicative, and problem-solving skills. Perhaps most importantly, from a developmental perspective, your child is now able to use foresight and internal mental representations, that is, to think "inside one's head" as opposed to relying on external sensory information and feedback. The child becomes a bit drunk with new-found power, and exercises it at every opportunity. Putting this ability into effect is how your child becomes an independent and autonomous person.

Your child has no choice but to seek power and control at every opportunity toward the development of an individual and autonomous self. Your child is still a baby, however, and hence quite limited in just how she obtains power and control. Opposition and defiance are the two standard tools.

Provoking a response from you is another popular device. While you would think that carrying on and getting excited is aversive to the child, let's look at this from the child's perspective. You are not an ordinary person to your child, but an omnipotent superhuman being larger than life. Think how very powerful it is for this little person to have such a tremendous impact on this great big powerful person. One or two simple behaviors, and fireworks fly. It's like throwing a pebble into a lake and getting a huge splash: You will continue to throw the pebbles if such minimal effort yields such enormous gains. Having the ability to get you upset is very powerful. This may help explain why your child continues to do things for which you punish the child: The gain outweighs the cost.

You can use this perspective to understand and change some of your child's behaviors. One can imagine the preschooler with a ration card for power and control. Rest assured that the child will get her ration of power and control, as she is developmentally driven to do so. While we can't control these age-appropriate strivings, we can control how the child attains his goals. Either she will achieve success by opposing, defying, or otherwise provoking us, or because we provide opportunities for the child to have some control over his own destiny.

Look for opportunities for your child to make choices. A popular strategy is the "choice of two", in which you provide two alternatives and your child chooses from among them. For example, "Do you want cereal or pancakes for breakfast", "Do you want to wear your blue or red sneakers", etc. Open-ended choices are too vague and unstructured, which can make a child anxious. If you choose the parameters, then your child will not have ice cream and cake for breakfast or wear a plaid shirt with striped pants. You are satisfied with whatever the child chooses, and the child has a feeling of control. Nobody loses.

So what do you do when the child, given the choice of cereal or pancakes, chooses ice cream? You calmly and quietly repeat the original choice, "Do you want cereal or pancakes for breakfast". Don't get excited, don't provide lengthy and animated explanations, in short, don't display any fireworks. If you continue to calmly repeat the choices without the fireworks, then the child will stop the fireworks too. Negotiation and compromise are okay too, teaching our children critically important life skills as well as showing them respect and giving them some say in their destiny. Don't get hung up on showing the child who is boss, because if you are drawn into that conflict, you've already lost.

The Purpose and Function of Your Preschooler's Behaviors

If you think about what you hope to gain from this book, chances are you want to change some of your child's behaviors. You want to increase this behavior, decrease this behavior, etc. Identifying a color, saying hello to Grandma, not hitting, eating fruit and not dirt, putting toys away, not throwing toys, using the toilet and the bed, these are all behaviors. If we use a systematic approach, then we can change behaviors.

It is important to realize that almost all of your child's behaviors have a purpose and function. A positive behavioral approach works to understand the function in order to change the behavior, because you really can't effectively do the latter without first doing the former. In order to change a behavior, you have to first understand its function.

This is not a very difficult or time-consuming process. In essence, if you understand the context, then you understand the function. First, though, we have to concretely and explicitly identify the behavior we wish to change. To use the professional jargon, we need to operationally define the behavior, that is, to define a behavior that we can observe and measure. **Getting along with others** or **not driving me crazy** are not operationally defined terms; **taking turns** or **not hitting** are. It is also best to work on one behavior at a time.

Once we've identified a specific observable behavior to change, then we need to understand the context to understand the function. To do this we need to do a functional assessment, that is, to note what immediately preceded and what immediately followed the behavior.

When we consider this in the broader context of general setting (like mealtime, transitions), we begin to understand the function. We need to address the function before we can successfully change the behavior.

A favorite example occurred several years ago. A mother of a four year-old and a three year-old came to me and said that she wanted 20 minutes of peace and quiet to cook dinner shortly after she arrived home from work. What was happening at the time was that, while in the kitchen attempting dinner, the children sounded as if they were killing each other in front of the TV in the next room. The mother would go in, yell at them to stop, and return to the kitchen. This scenario repeated every few minutes.

After a brief discussion it became clear that the function of the behavior was to get the mother's attention and physical presence, two of the most popular functions of preschooler's more difficult behaviors. Often a parent will say,

"Nothing was going on before the behavior", which is often a tip-off as to the function. What immediately preceded the behavior (screaming) was no attention and no physical proximity; what followed the behavior was attention and physical proximity.

The setting event in this example is an especially important one. After being separated all day, the mother greeted her children, put them in front of the TV, and then did what she had to do. Reunion is important for children after some separation, and will drive a strong need for attention and physical proximity. Many children will not rest until this need has been fulfilled. The procedure here is to provide a brief interval of undivided attention for a brief interval upon reunion, say 10 minutes, before you go about you business. The trick is in providing 100% of your attention; anything less is compromised attention and will not fill the child's need.

So back to the example. What I had to tell the mother was that I could not get her the 20 minutes, because that expectation was not developmentally appropriate. What I was able to help her achieve was a very pleasant preparation of dinner by including her children. After a brief reunion of 100% attention, the children then helped their mother prepare dinner. Attention and proximity were attained (the function), but the screaming had stopped (the behavior). Dinner preparation became a truly pleasant experience for all involved.

You need to do a functional assessment in real time as opposed to hindsight. In our preschool, after we operationally define one specific behavior, we keep a simple chart of antecedents and consequences. Every time the target behavior occurs, a designated person immediately goes over and writes down what happened 5-10 seconds before (antecedent) and 5-10 seconds after (consequence) the behavior, as well as what was going on at the time (setting event). After about a week of this information gathering, trends usually become readily apparent.

The same behavior can have any of a finite number of functions. The typical functions are attention, escape, tangible gain, power/control, or a desired sensation. For example, the child who gets up and runs away from the dinner table may be doing so to get your attention, to get away from an unpleasant situation, to get something he wants, or for the joy of moving. We would respond differently to running from the table for escape than we would for running away for attention, e.g., we would examine why the situation was uncomfortable for an escape function and we would not respond with a great deal of attention for undesirable attention-seeking behaviors. Understanding the function tells us what to do, so that we can be that much more effective in changing our children's behaviors. Information is power, and gathering information about our child's behavior gives us the power to change it.

Chapter 10: Love And Respect

Raising a child who is loved is the utmost responsibility of all parents. A child is fragile and can be molded and nurtured according to the right principles. Parents need to teach their children about every aspect of this life beginning with the important aspects of love and respect.

We are a part of a world that is so vast that one lifetime might not be enough to explore it all. From the time we are born, we are surrounded by people, be it family members, friends or strangers. How we interact and make a bond with them determines who we are as a person. If we talk to others politely, in a soft manner, they'll be more likely to be attracted to us and choose to be around us. On the contrary, if we are rude to them and say inappropriate comments, they may not want to associate with us.

A child needs to learn the importance of love and respect. Love being the key to all other aspects needs to be showered unconditionally towards children. A child who is treated with love and care is more apt to feel secure about things and is more willing to treat others in the same way that he has been treated by his parents. Children who are not loved and are disregarded by parents often choose the wrong path and vent their frustration on others or even their parents. A loved child is most likely successful in positive ways and doesn't readily associate with negativity. However, unconditional love sometimes has a tendency to spoil a child and balancing this with respect and moral values is equally important.

Everyone needs to be treated with respect and love. As the famous saying goes, what you give is what you receive. If we treat everyone with respect, that's what we'll get in return. On the other hand, if we display negative behavior and disrespect others, this is exactly what we'll get in return. This will impact our image and make it difficult for others to trust us and continue to give us love and respect.

There are many small ways in which children can learn to respect and love others. For starters, you should not allow your children to call you or other adults by their first names; teach them how each person should be addressed. In this way children will be able to recognize that the elderly and those in authority, who are worthy of respect, should not be called by their first names. Eventually, children will develop the ability to differentiate between a respectful attitude and a non-respectful attitude.

In addition, children should be taught to listen to their parents and respect their commands. For example, if your child is playing outside with other children and despite really enjoying playing, they should listen to you when you call them inside for whatever reason. They should not be stubborn and refuse to come inside and misbehave towards you (in front of other children); if they do, parents should teach them that they should honor what their parents ask them to do.

Health and Nutrition

Health and nutrition go hand in hand. To provide ultimate nutrition for children, parents need to keep a balance between healthy eating and not-so-healthy eating. Children are most likely to be more attracted to junk foods like chips, soda, candy, etc. Though, these foods may give them satisfaction for the time being, they may have detrimental effects on their health if not eaten in moderation. Health is the overall physical and mental well-being of a person. Parents should encourage their children to play outside in the backyard or park, either with siblings or neighboring children. This way they have a fun time and also learn to be independent and productive.

Consistently having good nutrition at every meal is a foundation for a healthy childhood. Parents should focus on a healthy lifestyle for every member of the family. If they discover that their children have the tendency to be more inclined towards junk food at the expense of ignoring the healthy alternatives, parents should take a look at their own eating habits and reduce junk foods in their own diet as well as in their children's. Some suggestions would be to get rid of sugared drinks like soft drinks, give close attention to portion size, and increase physical activity which will help their children to live healthy lifestyles now and in the future.

To incorporate better nutrition into their children's diets, it is important to include fresh vegetables and fruits at mealtimes.

Also, whole-grain bread and cereals, dairy products like cheese, yogurt, and milk along with high protein are necessary daily components of healthy eating.

The basic of healthy nutrition simply means choosing healthy alternatives from amongst the many choices that are available. Children have the tendency to be more attracted to unhealthy junk foods, and therefore, it may not be possible to completely eliminate these foods completely from their diets. What is possible, however, is that you can control the intake, i.e. you can impose a limit on the amount of junk food calories your children are allowed to have. This way they will be able to enjoy what they eat, but in moderation without leading to overly bad effects on their health.

Along with choosing healthy alternatives for your children, it is also important that you pay close attention to portion size. Initially, you should determine the portion size that would be fulfilling and healthy to avoid instilling a general tendency to overeat. Overeating is never good for health, even if the foods that are overeaten are healthy. Set a routine for your child to have 3 meals every day or 5 smaller meals throughout the day. They should have a meal when they feel hungry, even if it's not the scheduled time for breakfast, lunch or dinner.

In summary, parents play a strong role in setting up a health and nutritional pattern for their children. Likewise, it is their responsibility to instill the capability of identifying what is good for their health and what is not.

Chapter 11: Access And Usage Of Touch Screen Device By Children

Introduction of the Study

We are in the stage of touchscreen generation and Internet connectivity. Tablets, computers, mobile phones, gaming consoles, and even appliances are now powered by touchscreen technology and capable of connecting to the Internet. Who wouldn't want a touchscreen device? These devices are really user-friendly and often do not require a keypad, keyboard, or mouse to operate it. Even a disabled user can easily operate a touchscreen device with the use of one hand. Users with arthritis also find this technology helpful than traditional keypad and mouse. Even 3-year-olds can operate touchscreen devices without receiving proper training.

Each adult in my family, myself included, own a smartphone, tablet, and personal computer or laptop. And we can't deny that a grand majority of people all around the world, especially those who live in urban areas, own one or more of these devices that are capable of connecting to the Internet and have a liquid-crystal display (Hereafter, LCD) touchscreen.

In addition, these devices have the potential of increasing the speed of a task when compared to the traditional way of the mouse and keyboard. Using a mouse requires you to drag the mouse pointer, then point, and click. While for the touchscreen device, you only need to point by touching. The absence of a keypad, pointing device, and wires greatly reduces the size and weight of these devices, making them extra handy. It also reduces the cost of the device and makes the more comfortable. For example, a touchscreen laptop that is capable of detaching the keyboard is more mobile and comfortable than a laptop with an attached keyboard. Touchscreen devices have helped make our lives much easier than before and I appreciate the endless benefits they give.

As the mother of a 4-year-old girl, I quit my office-based job and began to work at home as a writer so that I would be able to take care of my child and monitor her growth. Moreover, I can say that as an owner of Google Android Nexus 7 and a touchscreen tablet, these devices have helped me tremendously in my parenting. As an example, I downloaded an application that taught my daughter how to sing the alphabet and an application that teaches her to familiarize herself with the counting of numbers.

I did not have to teach her how to use the application and only instructed her to play and sing along with the game. She managed to learn with her own style of random touching. Along with the first application, I also introduced her to another application in which toddlers are taught songs and how to dance along to songs, one such song being the ever popular "Twinkle, Twinkle Little Star." Thanks to the help of this application, my child and I had endless fun singing and dancing together, thus our bond was strengthened.

However, it is no secret that 4-year-olds can get bored quite easily if the things they do are constantly repetitive. Thankfully in today's modern society, there are endless types of educational games or applications that are available to us that help combat this issue. For example, I have also saved for my daughter movies like Barney and Pocoyo whose focus is teaching good manners and right conduct. But as with many things in life, we must find a proper balance. The problem I have noticed with my child watching these movies is that she tends to lie on the bed and watch for too long without communicating with me. This I believe can become an issue for her physical, communication, and social growth. Yes, I can say touchscreen devices are easy to use and helpful in aiding parenting in many ways; however, we cannot deny that these devices can sometimes easily eat up too much of our children's time when their screen time is not being properly monitored. This concern of mine led me to do some research, and the following is my presentation of the findings.

Background of the Study

A research survey conducted in the United States of America from Common Sense Media and Michael Cohen Group (MCG) release in Feb 2014 found that, from 2011 to 2013, the percentage of children with a smartphone mobile device at home increased from 52% to 70%. Children 2 to 8 years of age in households with at least one touchscreen device revealed that 36% had their own device and furthermore, families at all income levels own touchscreen devices nowadays. In addition, children are now choosing to play more with touchscreen devices than with traditional toys.

This suggests that touchscreen devices are more entertaining to children of this generation than the traditional toys we adults played with in the absence of advanced technology. Overall, this could also signal the end of traditional toys for the incoming generation. This study also concluded that children access in touchscreen device is also high. According to the research conducted by MCG, some of these children own a touchscreen device at the young ages of 5 to 10 years old.

For further study, the survey includes a list of activities in which children use the touchscreen device. The children from ages 12 and below are used for reference. The result, touchscreen device is more often used in playing video games, which I think is slightly unhelpful. However, the second highest use of the touchscreen device is aimed at learning which is beneficial to children's development.

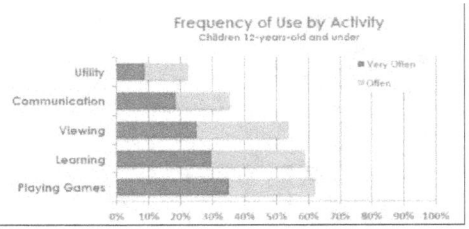

If we further breakdown "Playing Games" by type, the results shown are encouraging.

The most frequently played game type among 12-year-olds and below was "Educational" and the second highest was "Music." Music can be educational, such as nursery rhymes for babies. The third highest game type is "Free Play," which can include educational, musical, or a puzzles type of game. Lastly, the "Puzzles" game type comes in at fourth highest. Therefore, the top four frequently played game types by children 12 years and under are helpful for their growth development.

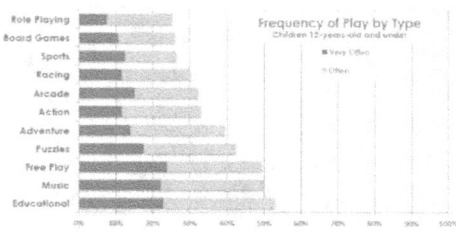

On the other hand, if you sum up the values for the games "Action," "Adventure," "Arcade," "Racing," "Role-playing," and "Sports Games," the end product result is higher than the educational games. These types of games could be harmful to a child's development. For instance, a 5-year-old child who plays Grand Theft Auto on a tablet device could potentially absorb that stealing and killing are morally correct. However, according to Dr. Romeo Vitelli, Ph. D. in psychology, violent video games have proven scientifically to have no evidence with the increase in violence of a person to others.

How, then, can we differentiate touchscreen device use for our children? Can we say that a touchscreen device is a toy? A survey conducted by MCG wanted to analyze what parents had to say about this, so they were asked, "Are touchscreen devices a toy?" and they could only answer with "Always," "Never," and "Sometimes."

On the above, we can see the results of this survey. If I were to answer this, I would pick "Sometimes," since most of the children use a tablet as a toy, especially children that are under age of 8. While the 9-year-olds and above tend to use tablets for educational purposes such as reading books for school. Some schools prefer softcopy of a book rather than hardcopy, especially subjects related to science. Furthermore, most students use a tablet or computer for research, communication, and socialization.

In another MCG research survey, parents who have 2- to 8-year-old children were asked about how their children access the touchscreen device. According to the research, N being the number of respondents, 553 or 52.2% of the respondents said that children could gain access by borrowing parent's touchscreen devices. Moreover, 385 or 36.4% of the parents responded that their child actually owns their own touchscreen device. It is also sad to see that only 27 or 2.5% answered touchscreen device use in school and daycare settings.

Another survey gathered information on how much time their 2- to 8-year-old child uses touchscreen devices. A majority answered that touchscreen device used by the children should be for a session length of 11 to 30 minutes, which is positive. However, there are still 273 and 33 respondents who feel that session lengths over 30 minutes are appropriate. According to MCG, the higher the age of the children, the higher the time usage of a touchscreen device and the more the family owned touchscreen devices, the higher the session length.

Conclusion for the Chapter

Thus, in this chapter we can conclude that in the United States of America alone, most of the children are exposed to touchscreen devices. This is definitely a growing trend and 2 years after the survey was done, numbers are increasing. Many online newspapers, magazines and parenting forums are consistently discussing and educating the parents. Children prefer using it as a toy rather than using traditional toys. The touchscreen device is commonly used by children for games and learning purposes. It can be neither an advantage nor a disadvantage to young kids.

Moreover, parents were asked, "How much time session does your child or children use the touchscreen device?" The result depended on the age and number of touchscreen devices the family owned. We saw that the higher the age and number of owned touchscreen devices, the higher the time session length the children used the touchscreen device. Which leads us to the next topic, what are the benefits and the negative issues that arise in children using touchscreen devices?

Chapter 12: Dealing With Power Struggles

We will look at essential steps that will help you adequately deal with power struggles that start as early as when your child is two years.

Side-Step the Power Struggle

A father once asked their four year old son to go to bed as it was their bedtime. "No", the child replied. The father then asked his son, "Which story would you want me to read for you during bedtime?" The child was very excited that he could choose the story he could be read and thus asked the father to read him his favorite story. The child even forgot about how he initially did not want to go to bed. As a parent, you need to learn how to side-step the power struggles; this is the first step of dealing with power struggles. What next now that you have sidestepped a power struggle?

Offer Choices and Not Orders

After side-stepping the power struggle, the next thing you need to offer is choices. In the above example, the father offered the child the choice of choosing which story he could read him for bedtime of which the child obliged and forgot that he did not even want to sleep in the first place.

You need to remember that choices should not represent one alternative as a punishment. For instance, telling your child, "Go to bed now and I will ready to you your favorite story or if you don't want to go to bed now, I will not read to you your favorite story."

Find Useful Ways of Giving your Child Some Power

Each time you are in a power struggle, you can always find a way of giving your child some sort of power in the particular struggle. For instance, if you are having a hard time having your younger son putting their dirty clothes in the hamper; why not keep him in charge of ensuring that everyone has their clothes in the right hamper? You will be surprised that you will no longer experience a power struggle in that area again.

Why Not Even do the Unexpected

If you feel that the situation is getting out of hand and each of you may end up saying nasty things to the other, why not for instance, offer some sort of treat. Remember that this is not to reward bad behavior but rather a way to create a loving relationship with your children and create the perfect environment for discussion. You will be surprised at how easy it will be to deal with certain situations when everyone is calm.

Offer a Win-Win Situation

The problem with power struggles is that it always feels like one has to win and the other person has to lose. With a win-win situation, everyone feels that they got what they wanted. Remember that as a parent, you cannot afford to be rigid; flexibility is required and thus you would need to compromise on different situations so that everyone is happy. All in all remember that Powerlessness creates the need for revenge.

If a child feels overpowered, they will always seek to have that power again through revenge and thus they will hurt others and engage in behaviors that will ultimately hurt them. Your child could start abusing drugs and alcohol, become pregnant or even commit suicide just to get back at you. This is why even if setting rules and limits is crucial, you may just have to relax them as your child develops and matures. This is especially so as the child grows and is capable of managing his or her own life. Most teenage rebellion is because the parent became stricter as the child develops. As children grow, there is a natural notion that this growth brings with it more freedom and independence to make choices and decisions that reflect directly into their life. You should gradually ease up the rules and limits as your child develops and even then, only when he shows mature responsibility.

6th Principle: Foster Independence

Being a parent, you will be tempted to equate your child's need for independence with rebelliousness. While this is very common and it is very wrong. You should always aim to strike a balance between setting limits (limiting freedom) and giving your child some independence. You should not badger your child into conforming. There are five important components to autonomy:

*Picking your battles (the right battles)

*Preapproving the choices your child makes

*Praising the choices your child makes

*Lending your child a helping hand (thought wise) in difficult decisions

*Occasionally letting your child make bad decisions so he or she can learn from them

You should not micromanage your child's life. Intrusiveness may undermine your child's self-confidence.

7th Principle: Consistency is Vital

Your parenting should be consistent day in day out. Inconsistency is a major contributor to disciplinary problems in children. Your rules and limit should not vary from day to day, week to week; they should be consistent throughout the child's life up until the moment you gradually relax them. The easiest and best way to help your child develop good behavior is to make any of his or her good behavior a habit that he does not have to think about. The best way to achieve this is by being consistent with your parenting.

Additionally, you should formulate a family routine. A routine is essential to the effective functioning of any family. In addition, a familiar routine makes the child feel secure and safe because the child knows what to expect and thus feel more in control. Your parenting style should be consistent without being too rigid. Your consistent parenting should also be adaptive to any situation that crops up, which you should expect. Your consistency and flexibility are symbiotic and as such, you should always focus on your child's intent rather than his or her behavior. As a parent, there are things you will not compromise on or be willing to compromise on, which is very important. If there are rules you think supersede others, you should not be afraid to enforce them in an uncompromising but humane way.

8th Principle: Harsh Discipline is Out of the Question

There is no disputing the fact you must discipline your child. However, should punishment be the correct discipline? Many parents struggle with this question. Here is a known fact; there are only three ways to change your child's behavior.

-*Punish

-*Reward, or

-*Explain.

While we are still on the topic of punishment, I should point out that YOU SHOULD NEVER, EVER USE PHYSICAL PUNISHMENT. Let us look at it from a simplistic point of view. If I offered you a choice between two types of medication both equally effective, one with some side effects and the other with none, which would you opt for? Most of us would opt for the later. This is the same logic you should apply when choosing any effective form of punishment when deciding to punish your child. Of all the punishments a parent can employ, physical punishment is the worst and has the worst side effects. Using physical punishment creates more problems than it solves. One of the main side effects is aggression; excessive aggression, which can easily escalate to a point where it causes serious physical and emotional injury to the child. Physical punishment involves hitting, spanking, slapping, or any other punishment a child or you consider physical in nature.

Scientists, through numerous research studies have proven that there is a very strong link between physical punishment and aggression in a child.

Personally, I think the best way to encourage good behavior is to give rewards rather than punish bad behavior. I am sure there are times that will call for punishment of bad behavior; however, if you embrace rewarding good behavior, you will start to notice that your child would want to embrace good behavior not because they will not receive some sort of punishment but because they will be given something good. Over time, such good behaviors become good habits ingrained in the child.

Always remember that you should never be verbally abusive. The success or failure of a parent is partly dependent on the child's belief that the parent has the child's best interest at heart. In addition, I should also point out that you should never punish your child when you are angry. You should aim to cut down on any anger emotions such as screaming and yelling because as we have seen, children learn much of what they carry on into their adult life by observing the parent. Is there a right way to punish your child? A more prudent question to ask should be, is there anything such as effective punishment? While there may not be an ideal effective punishment, most effective punishments have five key elements in a specific order.

*Identifying the specific wrongful act

*A brief statement on the impact of the misconduct on the child's life

*An alternative suggestion to the objectionable behavior

*A clear and defined statement of the ideal punishment

*A statement of feasible expectations

9th Principle: Always Explain your Decisions and Rules

The guiding principles of every parent should be to succinctly explain and make clear their rules and the reasoning behind these rules. Additionally, you should always be clear about your expectations. Many parents may feel "out of breath" when reasoning with their children; there is no specific way to go about it. However, here is a guideline to help you on how you can use reasoning:

* For children under the age of 6 - Your explanation should be extremely reasonable

*For children between the age of 6-11 - Your explanation should be both reasonable and logical

* For children above the age of 11 - Your explanation must be three things: reasonable, logical, and consistent with your actions and other things you have said.

You should never resort to using the, "because I said so" cliché. Additionally, you should always aim to hear and understand your child's point of view. This is important because it is a sign of good faith on your part. It effectively shows your child that every decision you make regarding their life has its basis on logic rather that your opinion. Almost 90% of everything your child learns is from watching the parent rather than listening to them. Therefore, you should always make sure you admit your mistakes. It is better for the child to see you as candid and fallible rather than deceitful and fallible.

10th Principle: Treat your Child with Respect

Almost every parent consistently worries if their children respect them; only a few of them ever worry about treating their child with respect or showing their children some respect. There is a general misconception that respect between a child and a parent is only when they agree; this is not so. Contrary to this notion, the measure of respect is how the parent and the child behave towards each other during a disagreement. Treating your child with respect demands that you accord your child the same courtesy you would accord any other human being. You will not earn your child's respect otherwise.

Treating your child with respect also means that your conversations are two way. In one research study among adolescents and children, one of the top thing most of these children wished was different was; a parent who listen and talks to them. As a parent, you have to be alive to the fact that there is a distinction between talking to your child and talking with your child. In addition, you should not always assert your authority over the child despite being the authority figure in your child's life. Instead, do the following:

*Pay attention to your child

*Ask your child for their opinion

*Ask questions that require a detailed response rather than one-word monologues

*Be authentic (genuine)

*Do not interrupt your child

Moreover, there are some expressions you should completely wipe of your response database. One of these responses is the "do not talk back" response, especially in response to any question from your child. Some other responses include; "You will understand it better when you are older," "I will ask for your opinion when I need it," "Shut your mouth," or "children should only be seen but never heard." Every parent must sweep these habitual expressions out of their expression closet. At different times and in different scenarios, most parents are very restrictive. You should let your child act his or her age. After all, childhood should be fun.

Chapter 14: Your Child Doesn't Talk To You. Ever. About Anything.

Why you B*tch: After school, coming home from a family party or deciding on what to have for dinner is met with silence (or one word answers). As far as communication is concerned, this particular type of silence from your child is not of the golden variety.

Why the problem exists: You're setting yourself up to receive one word (or zero word) responses from your child based on what you are saying to them.

How to start Parenting: Three words; Open. Ended. Questions.

Try this exercise with the closest person to you (child, adult, co-worker) at this very moment. Ask them the following two questions:

1) Do you like going to the movies?

2) I haven't been to a movie in a long time, maybe this weekend I should go. Which movie do you think I should see?

Hands down, every time, Question #1 will provide answers such as "Yeah", "Kinda", "Sure", "Not really", "It's expensive." Question #2 will provide answers such as "Yeah, I haven't been there in a long time either! The last movie I saw...", "I'm not sure but I heard this one movie is good. My friends all said..." "I don't even know what's really playing. Should we look? I think I saw reviews for..."

Get it? An open-ended question far outweighs the information you would get from asking a close-ended one. To be clear, an open-ended question is a question that CAN NOT be answered using a simple "Yes" or "No" response. Before you ask your child a question, any question, consider this: Can they respond using a simple Yes or No? If they can, change the question or statement around so that their response MUST elicit a reasonable answer.

Drop this: How was school?

Ask this: Hey! Tell me one good thing and one bad thing about your day at school...

Drop this: Are you hungry?

Ask this: What would you like to eat?

Drop this: Is something bothering you?

Ask this: You seem sad. I'll be really quiet so I can listen, what is bothering you?

I like to coin this way of questioning as "Assumptive Parenting." Assume that your child has already answered "Yes" or "No" to what your question would have been, and instead dive into the nitty gritty of what you're really asking. Children are also more apt to share their days and stories with you if you are willing to share with them.

Parent: Hey Nick what's wrong?

Nick: Nothing

Parent: Oh, you seem sad.

Nick: I'm fine.

Parent: Are you sure?

Nick: Yes

Versus

Parent: Nick, I can tell you're upset, what's bothering you?

Nick: Nothing, I'm fine.

Parent: Yeah, I know when I get that sad I don't want to talk to people sometimes. Want to know what made me so sad the last time I felt that way?

Nick: ::Says nothing::

Parent: My boss said something kind of mean to me and it hurt my feelings. I didn't have anybody to talk to, but then so-&-so asked me what was wrong so I told them. I'm glad I did because I felt a lot better. I found out my boss was mean to other people too so it wasn't just me he was being mean to. Maybe next time I can tell you why I am sad, is that okay?

Nick: Nods head

Parent: Oh good, I'm glad I can talk to you just like you can talk to me. So what's bothering you?

The dialogue in the second scenario is much more approachable. The parent lays reasoning for sharing feelings, explains a similar situation and even asks for the child's permission to bring their next concerns to them so that the child can help. Obviously these situations and subject matter must be in the parent's discretion (Yes: Starbucks made the wrong drink No: You and your husband are having financial issues).

Chapter 15: Running A Household And Finding A Balance

There are a few tips that are extremely instrumental for single mothers in running a household. They have to take care of everything on their own with no one by their side. This comes with it's own joys, challenges and responsibilities.

Some of these tips are as follows

Effective time management:

Since you have to do everything, managing your schedule is very important. Keep a calendar handy and plan your schedule ahead to avoid last minute chaos.

Multi-tasking helps you save time, for example, cooking and chopping vegetables while watching television or unloading the dishwasher while waiting for the coffee to brew.

Maintain **a proper routine** at home. This also teaches your child the value of time management. At the same time, take time off during the weekends and enjoy with your kids. In this chaos, always remember to take care of yourself. There is enough time to do everything; you just need to manage it effectively.

Sometimes there can be an overload of work. You can ask your children for help. This inculcates healthy habits in them. It will also carve a path in making them self-sufficient at an early age.

Work from home: This is especially effective for women who have to cater to infants or very young children. There are a lot of **virtual jobs** that pay well too. You can consider one of these for the time being. These jobs will allow you to save some precious time, which you can spend with your child.

While planning your day, keep some time aside for some unforeseen circumstances.

Social life as a single mother:

Amidst all the pressure and responsibilities, do not forget that you have one life to enjoy. Do get involved in raising your children, but not at a cost of not living your own life. Remember the adage, "all work and no play makes Jack a dull boy". This hold relevance everywhere, whether you are a Jack or a Jill! Therefore, make an effort to have an active social life and do the same for your child.

Make time: Do not just keep yourself busy in office or with your child's upbringing. Make time to meet up with old friends.

Choose affordable activities: Are you one of those who don't socialize for the fear of spending more? **Socializing** does not always come with a tag. Choose activities that are in your financial reach and are fun at the same time. You can choose to visit a museum or watch a movie or make use of weekend discounts at activity centres.

Plan a trip to the zoo with your little ones. This can be super fun and you can spend some quality time with your child.

Take a small vacation or organise picnics with friends who have children too.

You may want to consider joining the dance class you always wanted to or learn guitar as you dreamed of. Pamper yourself and be happy with your situation. Only then you will bring up the child in a perfect way.

Financial Management:

Money saved is money earned. You might have been a **spendthrift** earlier, but being a single mother comes with its own set of responsibilities. Therefore, curtail unnecessary expenses; rather save for the future.

We shall learn more about financial prudence and all that you can do, as a single mother in the next chapter.

Chapter 15: Raising Your Children

Parenting is considered to be one of the most researched areas in the field of social science. The relationship between the parent and the child will always be reflected in the child's behavior, attitude and actions. Having a good relationship with your child will bring them to trust you more, to listen to your opinions and to align their principles with yours.

Parenting is where the core principles and values of a child comes from. As the popular saying goes, **parents are the first teachers and the home is the first school**. This is where the child gets it from first. And doing all of these things right will help you to become proud of your greatest achievement which is your children.

It all starts with disciplining your children. Your child needs to know and acknowledge that as a parent, you have a certain authority over them. Several conflicts between a parent and a child, no matter the age and circumstance, springs out from the rejection of the authority of the parent. Now as a parent, handling these confrontations would determine the nature of your future relationship with your child, especially during their teenage years. This includes the amount of respect your child gives to you.

The first thing you need to establish are the boundaries between you and your child. Several studies have shown that severe, oppressive and unloving discipline is dangerous for your child. However, some parents justify that oppressive discipline is a way of showing leadership and authority to their kids. This is absolutely irrational and unwise.

There are instances where a strong-willed child will want to challenge his or her parents intentionally. Usually, the child is not motivated by hindrance or inner aggression or anger within his or herself. Most of the times, this is just because the child wants to know where the boundaries are and who is available to enforce such discipline.

Now, as parents, you need to know how to set limits and boundaries and what to do when your child displays bold and rebellious behavior. This disciplinary activity must always take place in the context of love, affection and care. It is proven by research studies that children succeed best in an atmosphere of genuine love, guided by rational and consistent discipline. Do not depend your disciplining based on gut reactions that occurs on spur-of-the-moment confrontations.

However, too much permissiveness allows the child to abuse the authority that the parents impose upon them. It leads to disasters wherein parents find it difficult to adjust. The key is to constantly thrive to be strict but always be reasonable. This allows the parents to prosper a good relationship with their children.

Disciplinary action is not an attack on parental love but a function of it. Letting your child figure out disciplinary actions alone is abandoning your role as a parent. Suitable and proper punishment is not a violation of your undying love for your children. You do these for them to grow and learn from their mistakes.

To emphasize, the main objective of disciplining a child is to gain and maintain their respect towards those holding authority over them. This however, requires audacity, consistency, persuasion, thoroughness and enthusiastic efforts from the parents. It is no easy task but once you fail in this, life becomes uncomfortable for both the parent and the child.

Proper and loving discipline, when properly applied and instigated to your children, will always work. It stimulates loving affection, made possible by mutual respect between a parent and a child. In the long run, this will encourage the child to respect those possessing higher authority over them like their teachers and professors in their formative years making them responsible and positive persons when they grow up.

Good parenting starts with good disciplining. This will lead to foster positive traits to your child like independence, honesty, kindness, resiliency, cheerfulness, self-control, optimism and compassion. This will also help promote intellectual interest, inspiration and desire to achieve within your child. Most importantly, this will help your child from developing anxiety, depression, anti-social behavior, giving in to peer pressure and several psychological disorders.

However, your child will always try and test your patience at every chance they get a hold of. They will drive you crazy at times and test your parenting skills.

Sometimes it is intentional and sometimes it is not. There will be these power games played by your children and they can be quite gifted at it.

These games start as early as 12 to 15 months old, with some getting started at an earlier age. A common example is when your child starts to play with something and he or she puts it in his or her mouth and you shout "No!" That is an early stage of power game between a parent and a child.

In this stage, the child's power game is probably not a conscious process yet. But later on, two or three years after, it will be. He or she will be motivated to challenge his or her mom and dad whenever he thinks he or she can win the game. Whatever the instance, may it be a bedtime battle or a veggie-eating fiasco, you as a parent needs to win the battle for the sake of you and your child's health. Again, practice good disciplining and you will be right on track.

With the passage of time, these battles do tend to become more and more intense. From the simple afternoon naptime schedules to schoolwork not done at home. Some kids even put their parents through hell just by trying to regain power and win the battles. In the process, wounds are inflicted to the parents that may never fully heal over time, and vice versa.

It all boils down to power. The sense of power is very attractive to all of humanity, even to meek children. It is actually a very dangerous thing to acquire and possess with all of its perks and consequences. If power can be so damaging to mature adults who think they know how to handle it, imagine what it will do to a child.

One of the characteristics of those who obtain power at an early age acquires a fundamental attitude of disrespect for authority. It extends to any other person that is or will hold a higher power. However, parents should not retain every ounce of power over their children. Even with the risks it provides, self-determination is a basic human right, an innate one. It must be granted systematically to your children as to avoid further resentment and conflict between the two parties.

As parents, your goal is not to transfer power too early to your children, even if it takes you daily to that battlefield of power games. At the same time, you must not retain parental power far too long either. Do not wait for your child to forcefully tear the control right off you. Surrender it voluntarily in the right time to prepare your child for maturity. This will save you from a ton of conflict with your child.

This task sounds easy. But you, as a parent, knows better. There is no complete and proper formula in transferring power to your kids. Some parents even go through a trial and error stage wherein they go along as they deem and learn from the mistakes they commit, if there happens to be some mistakes. This happens to be one of the most subtle and tough responsibility in the entire realm of parenting.

Do not take your chances. Make sure that your disciplining is coupled with parental power. This way you get to teach your children proper values and traits including respect for authority. And when adulthood comes, surrender it to your child completely and trust that you have raised him or her well enough.

Chapter 16: Disciplining Toddlers

Most times, parents don't want to enforce rules, they don't want to discipline children because they don't want to be the villain. They don't want to trouble their kids. Well, what I would say is this. "Give them enough trouble, lest they would trouble you in the future" there are some few aspects you should know about discipline.

First, we need to make a distinct line between discipline and punishment. Jo Frost, in her Supernanny show presents discipline as well as punishment in her bid to manage the child's behavior. Discipline is a way to teach the child self-control while punishment is what a child receives when there is no self-control. As simple as that.

Why do toddlers need rules? Like everyone in the world, when there is no rule, there is no sin. Everything goes, a complete state of anarchy. Rules also serve as boundaries set for your child to make them think and act orderly. Since discipline is not the same as punishment, then we should keep it positive. Physical aggression is not okay, aim at teaching the child how to behave. As much as I would love to say this, I would also want you to understand me. This book isn't a holy grail or a map for toddler care. It is a guide, sieve what you think is useless. Discipline your child when you really don't want to. There shouldn't be any lapse. Although, you may feel that this is strict. I consider it not to be. Let your rules be your rules and don't make them hard.

Discipline vs Punishment

We have discussed little about this in the introductory paragraphs of this chapter, but that doesn't stop us from doing justice to the subtopic.

A 1985 study shows a correlation between what seems to be corporal punishment, stealing, truancy, aggression, hostility, and depression, lying and low self-esteem etc.

Now what is the role of punishment? Punishment, when focused on the wrong direction causes children to put all their attention on anger toward an "unfair" adult instead of learning responsible actions-the sole aim of punishment. In fact, punishment when channeled in the wrong way validates fear, intimidation, pain and even violence. Punishment can turn a parent into an executioner and can even escalate into battering. Battering could lead to mental, spiritual and emotional harm. In contrast to discipline which provides an avenue for dialogue and communication and teaches the child how to control himself in a social order. According to Michigan State University Extension, punishment and discipline are very different and have separate outcomes for children and distinct impacts on parents as well as caregivers. Discipline is not spanking or telling your child she is missing dinner, that's punishment. Now when a child is punished negatively, the information you giving him is this. "Don't let me ever see you doing that again! Or I better not catch you doing that again" which means the child can continue his bad actions but must not be caught. Then the child learns to be careful. This has never been and would never be a good way of managing behavior.

The word discipline is derived from the word disciple which means to teach. In this context of child relationship and responsibility, self-control is key. We believe that over time, children would take ownership of inappropriate actions and understand their consequence but can we wait till then? Punishment could come in the form of spanking, insulting, blaming or even humiliating. Barbara Coloroso eloquently describes three different types of parenting in her book entitled Kids are worth it! Giving your child the Gift of Inner Discipline (1995) She suggests that parents can either adhere to brick wall (strict), backbone (consistent in disciplining techniques) and jellyfish (relentless and inconsistent) style of parenting. Parents try to develop any style on their own which falls between these ones to foster and instill respect, warmth and good communication.

Fifteen Habits to Nurture Long-Term Child Discipline

Positive parenting requires positive discipline and this means your child should develop positive values as well as social skills. Please note that positive parenting should not be confused with letting your child do whatever he or she wants. Positive parenting involves parenting in a warm, kind and a very respectful way. Your boundaries should be firm and relevant. Consequences of each action should be reasonable enough. Providing a loving environment should be your goal as a parent. The more positive attention and encouragement you give your child, the more they will respond to you. Positive parenting also requires you to use a polite and respectful tone when communicating with your child. Here are the seven fundamental principles of positive discipline:

Tell children what they can do instead of what they cannot do.

Protect and preserve children's feelings that they are lovable and capable.

Offer children choices only when you are willing to abide by their decisions.

Change the environment instead of the child's behavior.

Work with children instead of against them.

Give children safe limits that they can understand. Recognizing their feelings without accepting their actions. Maintain your authority calmly and consistently. When children break the rules allow them to experience the consequences of their behavior.

Set a good example. Speak and act only in ways you want children to speak and act.

Avoid power struggles. Explain why a rule is set or why others are enforced/established. It is important to communicate and provide adequate details about the rule. Children are grateful for explanations instead of just saying "no".

Take timeouts when necessary. Timeouts are simply a break and chance or opportunity for you and your child to start over fresh. According to Kathy Lynn, author of Who's in Charge Anyway, "timeout is not a place, it's a state of mind."

Avoid being patronizing, insulting or verbally inappropriate (i.e yelling, blaming). This form of parenting will in turn decrease the child's self-esteem. Comparison to other children and favoritism also could negatively impact the child's disposition.

Enforce realistic expectation, consequences and consistent communication of behavior. Define fair, firm and consistent follow-through.

Model positive behavior (i.e. actions, behavior and communication).

React at a normal voice level, not out of anger, tiredness or other negative emotions.

Discuss clarity in rules and behaviors, verbally and non-verbally.

Involve children in some family rule making. The child, in turn will feel empowered and more confident.

You should know in the long run that effective discipline evolves over time. Such discipline should be very consistent as well as age appropriate. Sometimes, you could bring two contrasting ideas when you try to explain inappropriate behavior and still want the child the express how they are feeling. Their feelings may just be inappropriate and they don't know. Here, you need to have a good understanding of the reason or the motive behind every action. When you are resolving the true underlying issues and when making further preclude future problems and negative repercussions, you need this understanding.

Appropriate Discipline for Different ages

Below are appropriate discipline for different ages.

0-1 **year** old

A waste of time to discipline them, like some people say. But loving touch and gentle words. Whatever the baby does may not be to get at you. It is not to be naughty.

1-3 **years**

Children are full of curiosity and life. They learn by touching and trying things out. And most of the time they make a mess of using things. Toddlers enjoy doing things on their own and get frustrated when they don't have the skills. The following are appropriate discipline methods:

Keep instructions simple and make sure you take one lesson and a time.

Avoid battles. This happens when a child is having a tantrum. Don't struggle with him or her. Simple words like "You've had enough. . . Okay, let's get you down from your high chair" could go a long way.

You may want to distract them by engaging them in any activity of your choice, because most times they don't know the consequences of their behavior and how to change it.

3-4 **years** (Preschoolers)

Here, children fully understand most of the instructions given to them. They are really excited and they could be very hard to control. The following process can be taken when it comes to discipline:

Teach the child choices by showing him what is really meant by choices.

Make sure you think ahead and let your child understand what is coming. The seven steps of discipline as mentioned above must be followed.

5-12 years (Primary school)

At this age, the child fully understands all about himself. He knows his limits and rules, they see things from their own perspective. And as a parent, you need to explain the core of adult behaviors and feelings which may vary. As parents, you should know the following:

Make sure you discuss with your children a wide range of topics. And it is important you listen to their views. Don't force your ideas on them, because they are entitled to their own feelings.

Contact other parents, a tree cannot make a forest. Learn how they relate with their children. They may not serve as an example for you because we are not learning formula's which work anywhere in the world. They are beings and it could happen that they become unpredictable.

Inculcate the habit of solving problems in your child. Teach him to solve problems in good ways. This is a very useful skill and at this age, it is important for him to be a step towards learning self-discipline.

Chapter 17: Positive Parenting: What It Is And What It Isn't

We've all heard the old lament – wouldn't it be nice if each child came with an instruction manual? Yes, it would be! Unfortunately, that's simply not the way parenting works. Each child is unique, and there is no single, prescriptive set of parenting tactics that works for all kids in all families all of the time. And when it comes to positive parenting, there is no one, single framework of rules that tell us what it means to use positive parenting in the home. Rather, positive parenting can be thought of as a perspective from which parenting choices can be made.

Positive Parenting – What It Is

Put simply, positive parenting is a style of disciplining children that focuses on positive, rather than negative, behaviors and responses. Discipline is focused on finding solutions (rather than punishments) for misbehaviour, recognizing good behavior, and learning for the future rather than punishing negative behavior that has already happened.

Positive parenting fosters mutual respect between parents and children and encourages growth and communication, making them partners in success.

To fully understand positive parenting, an important distinction must be made between discipline and punishment. Discipline is the process of helping kids learn how to behave and self-regulate.

Punishment is one form of discipline that involves giving a negative consequence in response to undesirable behavior. Punishment aims to decrease undesirable behavior by giving children negative experiences physically, emotionally, psychologically, or socially when the misbehavior occurs, so that they will be less likely to repeat the behavior in the future.

In punitive parenting systems, children behave because they are motivated to avoid punishment rather than because they understand the value of positive behavior for their lives. And although punishment can sometimes be used in gentle, healthy ways, in practice it all too often leads to negative consequences for children (and in some cases, outright harm), and can also contribute to parental stress.

Positive parenting, on the other hand, relies on mutual respect and teaching moments to help little ones understand the value of good behavior for their goals, relationships, and development. Children behave because they are motivated to act in ways that encourage positive responses and because they authentically understand and experience the benefits of good behavior.

Positive parenting is characterized by:

Focus on positivity: Positive parenting recognizes and acknowledges a child's good behavior, positive choices, and growing independence in regulating themselves.

Focus on the future: Positive parenting focuses on helping children learn for the future rather than making them 'pay' for what they've done in the past.

Focus on empowerment: Positive parenting seeks to empower children to make their own choices, rather than merely managing children so that they don't misbehave.

Focus on individual strengths: Positive parenting recognizes and draws from the individual strengths, abilities, interests, and desires of a child.

Teaching moments: Positive parenting views discipline and misbehaviour as opportunities for growth and teaching, rather than failures or shortcomings to be punished.

Natural Consequences: Positive parenting recognizes the value of natural consequences to misbehaviour.

Unconditional love: Positive parenting occurs in an atmosphere of unconditional love. In this atmosphere, children feel safe making mistakes, behaviourally or otherwise, because they know that even if discipline occurs, it is not because they are loved or respected any less. When children aren't scared to make mistakes, they are more likely to engage with the world around them and have more learning and growing experiences, further contributing to their sense of empowerment and self-esteem.

Child Centered: Positive parenting is child centered, meaning that parents work as partners with their children to help them construct healthy, productive behaviors, rather than simply handing them a set of rules and expecting them to comply arbitrarily. Parents act as guides, helping children learn for themselves by coaching them through their personal journey of growth and discovery. As children grow, parents help them to learn what behaviors are effective and appropriate for reaching their goals as individuals and succeeding as members of a family, community, and increasingly global world.

Cognitive: Positive parenting isn't just about helping children to approximate a standard of socially acceptable behavior. It also promotes cognitive skills and self-awareness as children learn to make mindful decisions, consider possible outcomes and alternative courses of action, and value and respect themselves and others as agents of choice.

Authenticity: Positive parenting relies on authentic communication between parents and children and focuses on helping a child develop his or her authentic self.

Positive Parenting – What It Isn't

Some may hear the term 'positive parenting' and cringe, envisioning children run wild in a house with no rules, no consequences, and no control. They may think that focusing on the 'positive' will leave children with no coping skills in the face of life's harsh realities, no respect for authority, and no backbone. They may fear that children will become entitled, emotionally weak, or unable to navigate failure.

In fact, the opposite is true! True positive parenting is very effective at helping children learn to be in control of themselves, make good choices, interact with others, and understand the consequences of their actions. So let's dispel some myths about positive parenting by taking a look at what it isn't.

Myth 1: Positive parenting means letting kids do whatever they want. Positive parenting does not mean having no boundaries or never telling children 'no.' In fact, positive parenting can involve as many boundaries and 'rules' as other, stricter forms of parenting – the difference is in the response of parents to children who break the rules or who can't have something they want in the moment.

Myth 2: Positive parenting let's kids 'get away with' bad behavior. The problem with the idea of 'getting away with' misbehaviour is that it assumes that children should be punished – that they must somehow pay for their 'crimes.' This philosophy can too easily become reminiscent of the penal system, and often leads to a disconnect between the behavior and the punishment. Positive parenting seeks to reinforce children's understanding of the relationship between behavior and consequence. By focusing on authentic consequences with clearly communicated purposes, children learn how to be more successful in the future rather than paying a penalty for a misdeed.

Myth 3: Moms and dads who use positive parenting are more interested in being friends than parents. Positive parenting does encourage connection, partnership, and even friendship between parents and children.

However, positive parenting is not about sacrificing the role of parent in favour of being best buds with the little guys. Positive parenting is a proactive parenting approach that involves conscientious effort and mindfulness of one's role as a parent who is responsible to teach and nurture children.

Myth 4: Positive parenting fails to teach kids how to handle disappointment and conflict. In fact, positive parenting is an excellent resource for teaching children how to handle disappointment and conflict. Because positive parenting is conscientious, hopeful, and focused on problem solving, utilizing personal strengths, and identifying alternative possibilities, children can learn to put disappointment and conflict into perspective and make choices to help them solve problems or come to terms with alternatives.

Myth 5: Positive parenting means sugar-coating the realities of a child's misbehaviour. Positive parenting does not mean pretending that a child's misbehaviour didn't happen or minimizing the seriousness of a behavioural problem. Rather, it means helping children to recognize the consequences of their actions, learn for the future, and move on. An emphasis on a child's strengths and positive choices does not mean ignoring misbehaviour when it occurs – rather, misbehaviour is seen as a teaching opportunity and a chance to express love and instil hope for the future.

Myth 6: Positive parenting encourages entitlement. Positive parenting does not encourage entitlement – far from it! Positive parenting encourages children to take responsibility for their choices and the consequences of their choices.

Children learn to see the connection between actions and consequences, promoting a realistic, logic-based picture of how the world works.

Myth 7: Positive parenting means praising children all the time. The truth is that positive parenting espouses authentic communication that is delivered respectfully and yes, positively. However, that doesn't mean offering false praise, inflating a child's ego, or praising children 24/7. Children will eventually pick up on praise that is inauthentic or unearned, and when they do, praise begins to lose its value. Positive parenting recognizes this and seeks to praise children authentically, for real accomplishments.

Positive Parenting: An Example

It can be helpful to take a quick look at a real-world example of positive parenting in action.

Mary, a young mother from Nevada, gave her three children, aged 6, 5, and 3, ice cream cones for a snack one afternoon. The oldest, Marissa, became upset when her ice cream fell off the cone onto the table. Distraught, she shoved the blob of ice cream onto the floor, threw her empty cone after it, and began to cry.

At this point, some parents may have responded by yelling at Marissa for making a mess, sending her to her room, giving her a punitive time out, or given her some other form of punishment for throwing her ice cream on the ground. Let's look at how this situation could be handled from a positive parenting approach:

Instead of merely reacting to the sudden mess and angry tears, Mary chose to respond. She got down on Marissa's level and said, 'Man, I hate it when ice cream falls down like that! But we don't need to throw things and cry. That won't help us get more ice cream. Can you try again?'

Marissa calmed down and asked politely for more ice cream, to which Mary responded by dishing some up while asking Marissa to clean up her mess. Mary also praised Marissa for finding an effective, appropriate solution to the problem. Mary then took the teaching moment a step further by asking all three children to work together to come up with ten more ways to solve the problem of ice cream falling off the cone.

They began to giggle and get into the problem-solving activity, with ideas ranging from picking the ice cream up and pushing it down further into the cone, to pre-emptively taping it in place!

In less than 10 minutes, Mary was able to:

acknowledge and validate her daughter's distress

point out that the behavior was unhelpful

help her daughter problem-solve a more successful strategy

enforce a real-world consequence (cleaning up the ice cream)

praise her daughter's success

get all three children involved in a fun, solution-finding activity that helped everyone learn

Through positive parenting, Mary was able to turn a potential tantrum into an opportunity for Marissa to identify and practice good behavior, and for all three children to have fun together and build their relationships.

Who Benefits from Positive Parenting?

The easy answer? Everyone! Children benefit from positive parenting by learning to take ownership of their behavior. As they begin to understand the connection between behavior and real-world consequences, they become empowered as individuals capable of affecting their own reality in ways that make sense. Because positive parenting creates a safe environment for making mistakes, children are able to experiment with the world around them without fear of losing parental love or respect.

Further, because positive parenting relies on good communication and a mutually respectful parent-child relationship, children can experience increased connection and satisfaction with their parents and other family members. Parents benefit from positive parenting for many of the same reasons. They often experience increased connection and satisfaction in their relationship with their child as they work to improve communication and take advantage of teaching moments. Positive parenting encourages parents to respond rather than react, which in turn can give parents a greater sense of control in difficult situations. Positive parenting is effective, which can lead to less stress in the home over time as children learn to behave appropriately.

Communities also benefit from positive parenting. Children who grow up in positive environments of unconditional love, emotional safety, and personal empowerment are less likely to experience depression, substance abuse, and unemployment as adults. They are also more likely to pass adaptive behaviors on to their children when they have their own families.

As you can see, positive parenting has many benefits. However, this isn't a one-size-fits-all approach. As discussed earlier, positive parenting is a perspective rather than a prescription. There are many techniques and strategies that can be applied from this perspective, and not all of them will be right for your child. We'll get into some of these practical applications soon, but first, let's set the stage by discussing how to become a peaceful parent.

Chapter 18: Battles To Overcome And Points To Ponder

Once the rules have been laid out, do not be complacent just yet. The following are few of the most common issues that you and your child would have to battle as he/she grows up.

1. The Need to Look Beautiful/Handsome

Blame it to the glitz and glamour of many advertisements. You see it every day, experience, and you just can't escape it. Neither can your child. So while you are busy with all the household chores and office tasks, your child pursues glamour magazines. While it seemed harmless at first, what most parents do not realize is that they actually shape a child's self-assessment.

What you can do as a parent: While looking good and pleasant is nice, setting your standards for your child is more important. This is not to advocate turning your children to meek wallflowers. But trying to look attractive is one thing, but turning a decent young man or woman into someone far from being his/ her true self is another story altogether. Your children's desire to look good is fine provided that you direct it. Don't make your children believe that they should be dictated by culture or what the society perceives as beautiful or handsome. He is who he is and does not need what the glamour advertisement says. Your child is beautiful/handsome just as he/she is.

2. The Need to Be Independent

Children of the 21st century are taught to be independent, think on their own, and make sound decisions based on what they feel is right for them. While this is totally true, it still misses the point that humans are all dependent on others – and your child is dependent on you. So while society teaches your children to be independent, you as a parent, needs to ensure that this is a natural phase and not a contrived one.

Children must learn and earn their independence.

What you can do as a parent: If you are raising a teenager and you think they are just impossible, the truth is, you just need to give them a little space. Understand that they are going through moody stages. Do not just give in and leave your teenagers be. The whole image of rebellion does not come from your child's biochemistry but is cooked up by this modern times and glamour advertisements. It is something that you and your child should not buy.

3. The Need to Acquire More

You may think this is undamaging but it will in the long run. Parents really find it hard to say "no" to their kids. It all starts with toys and clothes then move up to gadgets, a ticket to a concert, and many more. The problem is not really on having these stuff in your child's life. The real culprit is relying on these material things to make your child happy.

What you can do as a parent: If you are caught up in the viscous cycle of giving in to your child whenever he wishes to have something, remind yourself that should this continue, he will just end up pursuing material things in his life just to give him happiness even if he knows that it is only temporary. Assess the situation and ask yourself if your child really needs more toys, clothes, or gadgets. The answer will definitely be a "No", and you are very well aware of that. So act on that knowledge and stick to your decision.

4. The Need to Say "Yes" at All Times

Children wanting to belong would always find themselves saying "yes" especially to bullies. So if you see your child extraordinarily nice, generous, and sincere, there might be some problem along the way. Yes, every parent would want his child nice, generous, and sincere, but be warned that these wonderful traits are dangerous at some extent. Overly nice children are oftentimes people-pleasers. Generous ones give to the extent that they have nothing left and this might not work well in the long run. And, sincere children work hard to get everybody's approval and affection.

What you can do as a parent: Be sure you see these coming and assure your child that you really appreciate these traits. But here's the real problem: your child will have difficulty upsetting friends and find himself saying "yes" all the time. Teach your child to be nice but firm, say no and mean it. Teach him to act in a way that people will not take advantage of him and that being nice can be possible if he will leave up to the moral standards that you have set.

5. The Need to Be the Center of Attention

This is normal for young children, but they should not bring this attitude up to their teenage and adolescent years. Children, without proper guidance, often end up wanting to get the best that life has to offer and becoming self-centered in the process. Their lives are centered on getting things their way and relying on others to fulfill their wants and desires. They always want to be on the spotlight and frowns at people stealing the stage.

What you can do as a parent: Tell your child that life does not revolve around him. While it is good to achieve your goals in life and be recognized for the hard work, it should not get into his head and brag about such accomplishments. That Life should not always be about him and that one day, there will be this one person who is more capable and intelligent than him. Teach him these things so he will not end up becoming greedy of success and self-centered at all times.

Remember, you are your child's hero. Even if you are a single parent, you should act as a parent should be. If you are a father and you are raising your kids on your own, it is time to uncage your true masculinity. And it should be displayed through the moral exercise of authority. Your children will definitely need it. If you are a single mother, do not always unleash that emotional side. You should be tough yet with a soft side, firm with your decisions but often understands.

Here are some more pointers for the single Dads and Moms to properly raise kids of this generation:

Plan your rules beforehand – your hopes and dreams for your children are clearest when they are young. You should know exactly what you expect from them, what they are allowed to do and what is not. Write them down especially when you are just starting to parent a toddler. Have your rules inscribed and make it known to your child while he/she is growing up.

Have courage under fire – you sure will encounter loads of rumors and gossip, but remember to keep your cool. Show your children how you handle such idle talks so they will know how to handle these by the time they get into the same situation.

Be the leader that your child will follow suit – remember that you have far more experiences than your child. You have the ability to see the big picture and weigh the consequences of actions in a way that will be hard for your child. Children have the cunning ability to manipulate parents by throwing tantrums. So when your child tests your temper, put him in time out and ignore until he calms down. This very same technique can be done even if your child reaches his teenage years. If you need to ground him for a week or month, do so. Remember, lead, and don't let him. He sure will appreciate this when he has a family of his own and will ultimately run the house like you run yours.

Persevere– Parenting is a lifetime commitment. It does not stop after you send your child to college or walk her down the aisle. So stay engaged, spend time with your children as much as you can, be loving, patient, and consistent. Even if your marriage is doomed, stay with your children. At least for their sake.

Chapter 19: They See Through You

I know the title of this chapter is something you already know. But what happens is that what really hurts us is not what we don't know, it is what we know but fail to put them into practice. Take your time to think of the books you've read, words of advice you've heard from others, seminars and teachings that you've attended. How much of what you've learnt have you been able to practice?

This book isn't meant to teach you or tutor you on how you can raise your child for success. Nope, this book is meant to teach you how you can be a success then your children would follow. If you are a vegetarian, you don't drink alcohol and you treat your wife with respect, your children are learning to do that also. They see through you. They imitate everything you do. Everything! The way you walk, talk, eat, even the way you use the toilet! Yes, I am saying that from experience.

They imitate everything. They take note of your virtues. And I know you are aware of this. That is why you keep **hiding** things from them. Like when you want to take a smoke you have that spot in the back yard away from your kids.

Your children would become good and virtuous when you become good and virtuous. Parents who behave inappropriately in the presence of their children are deliberately telling the child that an inappropriate behavior is the right way to act. Most times they make these suggestive gestures in their presence. The child receives it and becomes spoilt. You should be careful of the impression you give your children. Effects from these impressions are as quick as a reflex action.

Parents of today have become fractured and restless and their speech keeps getting careless and hurtful and that is why children become bad. Kids are like computers; **Garbage In, Garbage Out**. What they see you do is what they process and that is what would build up behavior blocks in them. When a husband and wife use hurtful language a lot, it creeps into the vocabulary of the child.

The moral standard is not declining, it is practically gone. This is solely a result of bad parenting. Because every young adult has that potential to transform the world. Every child has the power to make the world a better place. And every parent has the key to create that perfect world. Without the proper guidance children become selfish and extremely self-centered.

One beautiful thing about parenting is that you can't run away from it. Parenting is mandatory. Yes, you may decide not to have children. You may decide to dedicate yourself to one cause so much that you feel celibacy is the best option. Whether you like it or not, parenting finds its way into your life. You may just meet that kid who would take you as a **mentor** or a father figure. There's every possibility that you'll become a **parent** someday. The values that you've been able to acquire though experiences, the virtues you've been able to obtain would build up that character block and all those things would be clearly projected into the life of the kid.

This is why parents should not fight in the presence of their children. That standard of conduct should come from them. If either parent makes a mistake or acts inappropriately, he/she should apologize. The children witness peace reign and they are happy.

Many people keep asking "How can I be a good parent?" when the real question should be "How Can I be a good person?" If you ask the wrong question, you get impractical answers. Become a better person and your children become better individuals. This sounds easy and simple. Yet we fail to put this into practice because it is **too simple.**

You should set that example for your kids. Yes, you convey the message. You keep telling them to do say **thank you** and not use the abusive words. But when it is your turn to act things out you become a complete opposite of what you preach. Children want to see their parents do whatever they preach. They learn quickly by imitating you. Manners are developed instinctively. What children need is that push or force from parents in form of **good behavior** to develop that right attitude.

Okay, they see through me. But I am nice to them and they still misbehave.

Caregivers and parents think that if they act nicely to a child or around a child, the child would act nice in return. It is called the "strings attached" technique. As an adult, you are familiar with this concept. You can relate with this concept of fair giving and receiving. However, most children don't really know what is going on. They are not mature enough to respond to you the same way you treat them. Expecting something like this from the child is unfair. Love and understanding are the two solid foundations of parenting. You should channel all the attention you use in **pretending** to be nice into showing love and understanding your child. Efficient discipline elevates self-esteem, self-respect, self-control and maintains that positive parent-child relationship.

It is very possible for you to act **all good** and your child still has some shocking attributes that would make you want to say; **oh my, where did you learn that?** Although the **parent factor** is a major contribution to the character make-up of the child. However, they face different stages of development and external factors affect their thoughts and ideas. Children are unique. Factors like temperament brain dominance, giftedness learning style and intelligence could make them look a bit **different** from you. If there are reoccurring traits in the child that do not **match** that of the parent, it is up to the parent to **see through the kid**. Understand these unique traits. There is every possibility that these traits are from you but life experiences have locked them up or erased some of them.

Conclusively, being a good parent requires a conscious effort to be a better person.

"Children who live with criticism learn to condemn.

Children who live with hostility learn to fight.

Children who live with ridicule learn to be shy.

Children who live with shame learn to feel guilty.

Children who live with tolerance learn to be patient.

Children who live in encouragement learn to be confident.

Children who live in praise learn to appreciate.

Children who live with fairness learn justice.

Author Unknown

Chapter 20: Plan Activities With Your Step Children

Just as it is important to encourage your step children to spend 1 on 1 time with their natural parents, it is also important to plan some of that kind of time with you. Doing something enjoyable with your step children will help them to bond with you. If there is a time when you don't have your own children, this makes it even more special to your step children.

One idea is to take your step children along shopping for gifts for their natural parents for their birthdays or for Christmas, or Mother's or Father's Days. This shows the children that you respect their feelings for their natural parents too. This will help you to earn their respect and enable them to see that they can actually love all of their parents. Many step parents share negative feelings toward their exes, but they fail to consider the children in the whole scheme of things.

What is a few dollars of your own money when it comes to earning the love and respect of your step children? Showing them (and your spouse) that you have consideration for the kids' love for them will go a long way to earning everyone's respect—perhaps even that of the exes.

Another idea of 1 on 1 time with your stepchildren is to find something that they really enjoy and do it with them. For example, if they really enjoy animals, plan a special day at the zoo when the other members of the family are busy with other things. What a great way to bond with your step children! And if you are short on extra cash, it doesn't have to be something that involves a lot of money. Doing crafts with them can be fun and can provide small meaningful gifts for others.

Include them in preparing meals or snacks. Not only does this provide time with you, but it also includes them in family activities. Kids love to help when it comes to doing positive and fun things. Make the little chores fun. Take them to the park or to the Mall (depending on their ages). Be involved with their activities. Support them when they play sports or take dancing lessons. Watch them dance and encourage them on the field. These are just little things to an adult, but they are extremely BIG to the kids.

As easy as this can be with your own children, you can make it easy with your step children too. Keeping them involved in the family unit will become very important to the stepchildren, and they will learn that they really DO have a special place in the family unit! This when your crew will become a well-blended family who loves and respects each other. It is not an easy thing to do, but it is well worth it in the end.

Chapter 21: Parenting Activities That Aid In Positive Families

Just like with the learning of any skill, you must practice it to gain perfection in it. Parenting is no different! Parenting activities are built to hone the skills you already have, as well as help you develop new skills. The activities outlined in this chapter will encourage you to set parenting goals, envision the future you want with your family, and give you some tools to deal with those challenging situations that will inevitably arise.

Behavior Chart Activity

Children naturally test their limitations because they crave the need to assert independence to control their environment. This activity allows parents to use limits to teach instead of punish. This activity is made to help you gain confidence as a parent and give you tools that are effective in setting limits with your child.

Jot out this checklist:

Make clear as to what behavior(s) is inappropriate and why

Offer choices of a consequence that the child can choose.

Allow time for the child to consider their choices and then come up with a decision.

Enforce consequences that are appropriate. Follow through with them.

Award points for achieving good behavior. Track them and come up with some type of reward system that they can redeem their points.

You will need:

Notebook to record your checklist and track successes

Behavior chart

Parent Goals Activity

It is important for both parents to set goals as a couple that they can achieve monthly. Instead of diving into harrowing details, look at the big picture. What long-term vision do you both have for your family, as well as for your relationship? Make a 5-year plan that allows you to reach those future goals. Here are some areas I suggest you work on as a couple:

Education

Community service

Financial, spiritual, physical well-being

Entertainment

Attitudes

Vacations

Spending time together as a couple without the kids

Discipline

Communication

Extracurricular activities

Brainstorm for each category above and choose 1-2 things to focus on. You want significant goals to work on, but make sure to create short-term goals as well. This activity gives you structure as a parent as you work towards achieving goals in your desired vision that you have for your family. It also encourages communication and helps both parents to maintain accountability.

Self-Care Activity

Many parents will go through a time that they lose their overall sense of self while they raise kids. This is easy to do, since the majority of their time is spent dedicated to just their children. So as a parent, if you feel frustrated and rather unfulfilled, you need to find some sort of balance by making time for yourself and time with your partner.

What to do:

Make a "feel-good" list of all the things you have wanted to do but just never have the time to do these days. Create a wish list of things you enjoy but don't do because you sacrifice them for the sake of your children.

Once you have a list, make it a priority to complete at least one of those activities per week. I recommend keeping a journal to jot down your feelings and thoughts and how those activities benefitted you and your family.

Partaking in activities that make you feel good and refreshed helps you to connect with your personal self and allows you to devote some time to bettering yourself.

This will not only shine through in your life, but throughout the entire family as well. When you feel good, you can give those "feel-good" feelings too!

Staying Positive Activity

Negative outlooks on life leave anyone feeling humdrum and down in the dumps. It's important to encourage the discovery of new way to be positive for the entire family. When you begin to take notice that you continuously think negatively, utilize this activity to get back into a state of positive and calmness.

What to do:

Sit in quiet place for at least five minutes. Focus in breathing, inhaling for five seconds and exhaling for five seconds. Hone in on the way your chest feels when taking in and expunging air. Repeat this rhythmic breathing and if thoughts come to light, acknowledge them but focus back on your breathing.

I suggest performing this activity at least once a day, everyday. It helps you to retrain your mind to think happier thoughts. At the end of each exercise, read off some positive affirmations that will help you to control chaotic negative thoughts. This will help you to release negativity from your body and mind and encourage relaxation and calmness.

Positive Parenting Activity

It is much easier to focus on behaviors that you do not want from your kids rather than the opposite. I have found that nagging only become a bad habit that usually just backfires on me as a parent. In order to encourage good behavior from your kids, you must learn to hone in on what they are doing right and reward them for good behavior.

What to do:

Pick a day during the course of the week to commit to yourself that you will only focus on the good behavior that your child does. Comment only on the positive things you see your child doing, instead of pointing out all the things they are doing wrong. If you do see a negative behavior, really strive to correct it in a positive way. Reinforce good behavior with the chart that was discussed at the beginning of this chapter. Every time your child performs a good behavior, reward them with a point on the board.

This activity can lead to a nice peaceful harmony in your household. You are encouraging your kids to behave the way you wish them to when you practice positive parenting strategies. Let's face it, everyone likes receiving good praise!

Chapter 22: In A Nutshell

If you try you won't succeed.

This is all about:

* setting compelling outcomes that you believe have value for you,

* committing to them,

* applying your skills,

* acquiring any new ones you need through modelling,

* just DO IT!

Personal note from me...

I decided to try and get my son to bed earlier so he wouldn't get so tired and grumpy. Needless to say, it didn't work because I didn't organise myself properly so he had eaten and done his homework after school. It was only when I committed to it and believed in it enough to organise myself, that it happened.

Personal note to yourself...

6. The map is not the territory

What this means is that how you see the world is different from how others see it. We all have different perceptions of our environment depending on our age, life stage, culture and experiences. To assume our perceptions are the only correct ones would be unecological in NLP terms.

This is ever obvious when you consider how your children see their world. Their map is very different from ours.

Their priorities are different and based on a very small map mostly involving them!

They have no or very little awareness of the bigger picture that we see and as parents we usually want to protect them from this, for a while at least.

Children inhabit a quite insular space centred on the home and school plus a small area of community. It is a world where they feel safe and loved, where the worst thing they can think of is that world changing.

Children fear change because so much is still unknown to them and they have no experience of it to reassure them that they will be OK.

When we encounter change we usually have something similar that we can draw on for reassurance and confidence. We can help children cope with change in the same way.

When our children need to make a change we can remind them of how well they have coped with changes they have experienced such as the birth of a sibling, moving to a new room, going on holiday and making friends, starting at nursery school and so on.

When you need to understand your child's map, instead of drawing on your own experiences of being a child (although that can help) ask them about it.

We can use metaphors to help children express their feelings.

Whilst asking a direct 'how do you feel about that?' question to an adult works reasonably well, it doesn't with children.

Ask children instead to equate it to something they are familiar with by asking them 'what is like joining a new class?' or 'who are you when you have to answer a question in class?'

Children will happily draw on characters they know from TV or video games, friends they know, animals or may even be able to equate it to another experience they have had.

To find out more, simply reflect back what they have said in question form. We call this using a 'clean' question.

So if your child has said that starting a new class is like being a small animal in a large scary jungle, you can say 'a small animal in a large scary jungle?'

Enter their territory by stepping into their shoes and seeing it from their viewpoint.

You'll find this easier when you spend time with them playing or watching their TV programmes.

When you read them a story and a character is expressing an emotion you think they might sometimes feel such as anger, sadness, jealousy or fear, ask them

-are there times when you sometimes feel like this?

-when do you feel like this character?

-what do you think this character could do about it?

-how would you help them feel happier?

Chapter 23: The Way Our Moms Affect Us

Sunday. Evening. My official holiday. I'm in bed, feeling a bit unwell. Suddenly, on my Skype, I see a client with a bunch of crying emoticons asking me for an urgent consultation. As a rule, I refuse to consult when I am ill. But here I understand that the issue is critical, and we talk on the phone.

I was instructing this client, let's call her Mary four years ago. After my instructor's duties had been over, we called each other several times. She is a wise person who wouldn't call in the late evening of the weekend to have a chat.

She is switching the camera on, and I see a tear-stained face. She begins telling her story. Her mother, who lives in another city, and relations with whom have always been complicated, came to her place. When Mary was 17, she went to London to enter the university, and since then, her love for the mother has been directly proportional to the duration and frequency of visits. After graduation, Mary got married and three years later had a baby. Mother took leave and traditionally came to help. Then the first conflicts occurred when the mother, quoting Dr. Spock, kept telling (quite toughly) that the child should have the freedom to shout in a cot, with arguments like,

'A child must know his limits – give him an inch, and he'll take a mile!'

Mother would even stand by the cot and physically would block the woman a passage to her child. But then, the husband intervened and said that he was taking leave and would help so that a mother can go home. Mother slammed the door, saying, 'Let's see what you will raise!' and ceased communication for six months.

I remember the story excellently. As an instructor, I felt useless. When you see a conflict with the roots in childhood, you know how the defense mechanisms against children's traumas switch on but can't help to solve them because the client has no resource to deepen into the pain, you can observe. Back then, I admired the deed of the husband, who came and put everything in proper places.

After childbirth, a woman is always seeking the protection of her husband. In my situation, my husband (now ex) passed me to his mother, knowing my attitude to her and supported her participation in our conflicts, persuading me that I should be thankful to her. I took it as a betrayal. I could explain everything to myself: the fact that he worked and did her best to help. But deep inside, I felt like a lonely warrior in the enemy's camp. You know, you either have feelings, or you don't. You can convince yourself to do everything, but at the same time, feelings always remain as they are.

And then mother came back four years later. No, she was coming for a couple of days earlier. My husband was always at home, and if she said something, this was done very carefully, and my client was able to endure these words. This time, a mother came for a week when the husband went on a business trip.

You know, my daughter lost cannon. She started to do things that I could never even imagine. First, I was embarrassed because of my mother's words: 'let's see what you will raise" were entirely justified. Then I started to realize that my husband had been away, and I was always in the fighting stance, which was transmitted to the child. I had enough brains to understand this. But tonight, it was the apogee...'

While listening to her story, I have understood that, besides the situation described by Mary, there is another side – the mother was expecting the unruly behavior from the child. As far as I have understood, she's a healthy and imperial woman, always with earnings; she was carrying her family on her shoulders, so she has a strong will. For such people, expectations from the others become a reality soon, and the position of a dominant female suppresses the will of the one she thinks of as of inferior one. And Mary honestly takes the place of a confused teenager who can only snarl without controlling reality with her intentions.

'The situation was foolish. We were sitting in the kitchen and talking. My daughter came in and asked for a drink. Mother made her a remark that adults are talking, and she's a big girl and can already help herself with water. But I got up and poured her some water. Then my daughter climbed into my lap and started attracting attention, shouting, and interrupting us. I know the roots — she wanted to sleep; she was tired. I talked little to her for the last few days, because I spent all my time with my mother. She keeps hassling me, like, my curtains hang wrongly, or my child watches cartoons. I feel myself wearing some protective armor. It is entirely clear that my daughter wants to get her world back, the world in which she lived, and also to return my attention.

Mother started reprimanding my daughter as she did to me in childhood rigorously and arrogantly. I got lost. My daughter first swung at her and said, 'You are bad, go away!', Then she jumped from my lap and rushed to the bathroom. But my mother didn't rest on her laurels.

She followed her, opened the door, and started demanding from my daughter to apologize. Here, I have to say that my girl is a fighter. She is very tender and expresses love brightly, but if she feels any injustice towards herself, she will stand to the end, and it is tough to break her will and cause tears. First, I was observing from the kitchen as a mother reprimanded my daughter while hovering over her. I had to interfere at this very moment, but I felt like I fell into a stupor. Then I heard my daughter crying, and started to shout something angrily. Mother rushed towards her and grabbed her. My daughter was struggling.

And at this moment, I exploded. I ceased controlling myself. It was pure rage. I told her to leave my child alone and put her in her place, saying that if she wants to raise someone, give birth to another baby. I was so angry that if she hadn't listened to me, I would have hit her. My look and my tone sobered my mother up, she let my girl go, and my daughter ran up to my arms. She buried her nose in me and started sobbing. We went to the bedroom. We were laying there for long. She asked me, 'When is she leaving?' She told me terrible things about what the mother wanted to do with her.

Her words made a hair on my head move, but I realized that I just had to listen. I heard the front door slamming. When my daughter fell asleep, I saw that my mother's belongings had disappeared, and she had gone into the night. I called her and heard an angry tirade that I am wrong in raising a child, that my daughter doesn't know any limits, that she is leaving with the first train, since I, instead of supporting her, indulge the girl's whims. And that it's all my fault. I'm a bad mother; I'm a bad daughter. Besides, I'm a terrible person, just because I hate another person so strongly now.'

I go into such details (although I tried to make this story as brief as possible) because, from time to time, I face such situations, but just in different interpretations. I won't set forth the whole conversation and my recommendations in detail, for it will be hard to put three hours of blamestorming on paper. I will focus only on the key issues here.

Conclusion

Your child is not the only one taking grip with this diagnosis. It's a really hard core to be in this situation but you always had to act decisively and accordingly for your child. You must show him strength and love. You must support every decision that he'll make and enlighten the path that he'll take. No one can understand him the way you do and no one will ever try to understand his fault except you. You are his hero and defender. He is a blessing that no one can impart. He may be born with this condition but he was created just like other child. He is special and let him to feel that he is.

When you feel that he is tired and restless, give him rest. Teach him how to be brave and patient. Tell him the difference between discipline and scolding.

Dyslexic child can be frustrating and upsetting but you, as their parent should teach them how to go on with life, how to travel alone and be dependent. Show them the pieces of their soul that they should take up and build.

Your child is the most precious gift that God gave you. No matter how imperfect his physical or mental condition is, there is the perfection that lies within.

www.ingramcontent.com/pod-product-compliance
Lightning Source LLC
Chambersburg PA
CBHW072005070526
44583CB00015B/1341